Connell Guide
to
Charles Dickens's

Hard Times

---

by
Uttara Natarajan

Contents

NOTES

Introduction

Hard Times is Dickens's shortest novel, but despite this – or because of it – it's not his most readable. Published in weekly instalments from April to August 1854, it was his first return to weekly serialisation since *Barnaby Rudge* in 1841. (The four novels in the interim had all been published in monthly parts.) Later, as a single volume, it lagged far behind his previous fiction in sales figures. Dickens himself complained that he had found the weekly format "crushing". As one contemporary reviewer, Richard Simpson, put it, "the story is stale, flat, and unprofitable; a mere dull melodrama, in which character is caricature, sentiment tinsel, and moral (if any) unsound".

Although contrary views were expressed by such influential commentators as John Ruskin and George Bernard Shaw, the consensus on the book up to around the middle of the 20th century remained more or less in line with Simpson's view. The novel was generally taken to be Dickens's worst: overly didactic, overly schematic, and overly dogmatic, all faults unrelieved by the genius for characterisation and the capacity for humour that mark his greatest achievements in fiction.

The turning point in the critical assessments was F.R. Leavis's praise. In *The Great Tradition* (1948), Leavis adopts the other extreme position, that *Hard Times* is Dickens's sole contribution to the great tradition of the English novel, displaying a moral seriousness lacking elsewhere in his more entertaining work: "It has a kind of perfection as a work of art that we don't associate with Dickens – a perfection that is one with the sustained and complete seriousness for which among his productions it is unique." The stature gained by the novel from Leavis's estimate, whether disputed or confirmed by subsequent commentators, at least ensured that it was no longer overlooked. Nowadays, if it is still not Dickens's most readable book, it is certainly one of his most read. The name of its principal character, long absorbed into the English vocabulary, continues regularly to be invoked as shorthand for a rigid adherence to fact.

Moral seriousness is not a recommendation to all readers. But whether *Hard Times* works for its reader or not, it's hard to deny its impact. This is Dickens in full battle mode, and the force of his outrage demands our attention. *Hard Times*, he told his friend and mentor, Thomas Carlyle, "contains what I do devoutly hope will shake some people in a terrible mistake of these days, when so presented". That the words "Gradgrind" and "Gradgrindian" have stayed in use as pejoratives, well into the 21st century, says something about his success in that purpose.

A summary of the plot

Book I

Thomas Grādgrind, recently retired from the hardware trade, is the owner of a model school, offering a modern, strictly factual, and Utilitarian education, in Coketown, an industrial town in the north of England. Among the school's pupils, Bitzer shows the greatest aptitude, and Sissy Jupe, the daughter of a circus clown, the least. Gradgrind has five children, Louisa, Thomas (Tom), Jane, Adam Smith, and Malthus. Mrs Gradgrind is feeble and silly, parroting her husband's opinions without understanding them, and barely participating in the upbringing of their children. Gradgrind's best friend is Josiah Bounderby, a banker and manufacturer. Mrs Sparsit, a widow who has fallen from former affluence, presides over Bounderby's household.

Discovering that her father has run away from Sleary's Circus, where he had become increasingly unsuccessful as a performer, Sissy opts to leave the circus and enter the Gradgrind household, so as to complete her education, according to her father's wishes. In due course, Gradgrind becomes Member of Parliament for Coketown. Sissy's poor performance in school leads him eventually to discontinue her education, but she remains in his household. His eldest child, Louisa, marries Bounderby, older than her by many years.

Bounderby gives Tom a job at his bank.

Among the workers employed at a factory owned by Bounderby is Stephen Blackpool. Stephen is married to a degenerate and alcoholic wife, from whom, lacking financial means, he is unable to obtain a divorce. He is in love with Rachael, a working woman, who returns his love and whom he regards as his moral and spiritual guide. Following a visit to Bounderby, Stephen makes the acquaintance of an old woman, later named as Mrs Pegler, who expresses a great interest in and admiration for Bounderby.

Book II

After Bounderby's marriage, Mrs Sparsit has moved to apartments at the bank, where Bitzer is now working as light porter. James Harthouse, a gentleman from an upper-class family, arrives in Coketown with a view to finding professional occupation there. He meets Louisa Bounderby, to whom he is immediately attracted, and quickly discovers that her only attachment is to her brother, Tom.

Because of a promise to Rachael, Stephen refuses to join the workers' union and is ostracised by his fellow-workers. He is subsequently sacked by Bounderby for criticising the way in which the workers are treated by their employers. Sorry for his ill-treatment, Louisa, along with Tom, visits Stephen to offer him financial assistance, and finds that he is about to leave Coketown to seek work elsewhere. Tom asks Stephen to wait for a message from him in the vicinity of the bank in the evening before he leaves. Stephen does so, but, receiving no message, leaves Coketown.

James Harthouse gains an intimacy with Louisa, in the first place by showing an interest in Tom, who has a gambling habit and is heavily in debt. A robbery is discovered at the bank on the morning after Stephen leaves Coketown and suspicion falls upon him. Mrs Gradgrind dies. James Harthouse, watched by Mrs Sparsit, tries to persuade Louisa to elope with him. Instead, Louisa flees to her father and, after confronting Gradgrind with the failure of her marriage and her life, collapses.

Book III

Recovering, Louisa notes the evidence of Sissy's beneficial influence everywhere in her father's household. Initially hostile to Sissy, she is soon reconciled to her. She remains with her father, permanently estranged from Bounderby. Sissy confronts James Harthouse and persuades him to leave Coketown for good.

Mrs Pegler is forcefully dragged into Bounderby's presence, in front of a large crowd of onlookers, by Mrs Sparsit, who has mistakenly associated her with the robbery. She turns out to be Bounderby's devoted and self-sacrificing mother, giving the lie to the stories of childhood abuse and neglect that Bounderby has strenuously propagated.

Rachael writes to Stephen, asking him to return to clear his name, but he does not appear. Taking a walk in the fields outside Coketown, she and Sissy find signs that Stephen has fallen down the Old Hell Shaft, a disused mine pit. A rescue party is formed, and Stephen is lifted out, to die shortly afterwards. Before he dies, Stephen asks Gradgrind to clear his name, and indicates that Tom has the knowledge to do so. Louisa and Gradgrind are convinced of Tom's guilt in the robbery. Sissy, by this time guessing the truth, dispatches Tom to hide at Sleary's Circus, then performing in a town near Liverpool. Louisa, Gradgrind and Sissy follow him there. Just as Tom is about to get away to Liverpool, he is apprehended by Bitzer. Sleary engineers Tom's escape.

Mrs Sparsit is dismissed from Bounderby's employment. Brief details are given of the future lives of the characters: Mrs Sparsit, at the mercy of a tyrannical female relation; Bitzer, taking Tom's place at the Bank; Bounderby, dropping dead some years later on a Coketown street; Gradgrind, chastened; Tom, dying just as he is about to be reunited with his sister; Rachael, tending compassionately to Stephen's wife; Louisa, remaining unwed and childless; Sissy, a happy wife and mother.

What is *Hard Times* about?

"What means this bitter discontent of the Working Classes? Whence comes it, whither goes it? Above all, at what price, on what terms, will it probably consent to depart from us and die into rest?" So asked Thomas Carlyle, to whom Dickens later dedicated *Hard Times*, in his influential pamphlet 'Chartism' (1839). To Carlyle, the spectre of revolution, raised by Chartism, the great workers' movement in Britain in the first half of the 19th century, loomed large. The blame, as he and Dickens and many other contemporaries saw it, lay squarely with the two systems of thought that had come to dominate social relations: Political Economy and its near equivalent, Utilitarianism.

The first phrase, broadly associated with the economic theories of Adam Smith (1723-90) and David Ricardo (1772-1823), was shorthand for the argument that national prosperity is best furthered by allowing industrialists to maximise profits, unhampered, paradoxically, by any regard for social good. Equally, the principle of utility or "the greatest happiness of the greatest number", proposed by Jeremy Bentham (1748-1832) – calculating value on a statistical basis – makes self-interest the automatic tendency of the individual and the sole motive force of human endeavour.

Both systems treat humanity en masse, rather

than as a collection of individuals; both, in their antagonists' perception at least, dismiss those aspects of human experience that are not quantifiable: imagination, creativity, our feelings for each other. Dickens's caricature Benthamite is

> "Thomas Gradgrind, Sir. A man of realities. A man of facts and calculations... With a rule and a pair of scales, and the multiplication table always in his pocket, Sir, ready to weigh and measure any parcel of human nature, and tell you exactly what it comes to." (I, ii)*

His practising Political Economist is "Josiah Bounderby of Coketown".

The accuracy, or lack of it, of Dickens's view of the systems he attacks has exercised a number of commentators from his own time to ours. From the novel's perspective, at least, this is beside the point. Only a few years prior to the publication of *Hard Times*, a revised model of political economy, based on a more sympathetic view of the working class, was proposed by John Stuart Mill in his *Principles of Political Economy* (1848), of which Dickens was certainly aware; later, similarly, Mill's *Utilitarianism* (1861/1863) set out a substantially qualified version of Bentham's, to include exactly those aspects of human experience – poetry, the arts, imagination – shut out in Dickens's

*Throughout this book, the numbers in brackets refer to the chapters from which the quotations are taken.

caricature. But the critique mounted in *Hard Times* is not to be addressed by revision or qualification. Dickens's fundamental objection, passing over the exact details of the systems that he targets, is to the mass model in any form whatsoever.

The fallout of treating people like numbers is the formation of the working classes into mobs. As Dickens portrays it, the mob is the dreadful alter-ego of that undistinguished mass of humanity so casually dispensed with by the political economists. Individually helpful and compassionate, as Stephen Blackpool describes his co-workers to Bounderby, as a collective, they become hard and unfeeling. Dickens's account of

JEREMY BENTHAM
ON POETRY AND
PUSH-PIN*

"The utility of all these arts and sciences, – I speak both of those of amusement and curiosity, – the value which they possess, is exactly in proportion to the pleasure they yield. Every other species of pre-eminence which may be attempted to be established among them is altogether fanciful. Prejudice apart, the game of push-pin is of equal value with the arts and sciences of music and poetry. If the game of push-pin furnish more pleasure, it is more valuable than either. Everybody can play at push-pin: poetry and music are relished only by a few. The game of push-pin is always innocent: it were well could the same be always asserted of poetry. Indeed, between poetry and truth the workers' union, easily manipulated by its unscrupulous leaders, is informed by the strikes and riots that erupted nationwide in the course of the Chartist movement (founded in 1838), a movement that sought – the first in the world to do so – to secure greater political rights for working men. Chartism finally petered out in 1848, the year of publication of *The Communist Manifesto* and only six years before the publication of *Hard Times*. In the 1840s, the fear of a workers' revolution in England was by no means remote.

To Dickens, mass theories and mass action are inextricably linked, entailing, alike, the loss of humanity. The counter to both is the recovery of the value of individual life. That value inheres in

there is natural opposition: false morals and fictitious nature. The poet always stands in need of something false. When he pretends to lay his foundations in truth, the ornaments of his superstructure are fictions; his business consist[s] in stimulating our passions, and exciting our prejudices. Truth, exactitude of every kind is fatal to poetry. The poet must see everything through coloured media, and strive to make every one else do the same. It is true, there have been noble spirits, to whom poetry and philosophy have been equally indebted; but these exceptions do not counteract the mischiefs which have resulted from this magic art. If poetry and music deserve to [b]e preferred before a game of push-pin, it must be because they are calculated to gratify those individuals who are most difficult to be pleased." (from *The Rationale of Reward* [1825]) ∎

push-pin was a simple child's game involving pushing pins around, sometimes on the brim of a hat.

human feeling, outside the parameters of the mechanistic models of human behaviour. In feeling – or, as Blackpool puts it, "drawin nigh to fok, wi' kindness and patience an' cheery ways" (II, v) – the self reaches out to the other. Dickens locates the sole and sufficient ground of moral action and social good in the individual's capacity to feel; his writing at once depicts, and plays to, that capacity. In this, *Hard Times* is like every other of his novels. In the fashionable parlance of today, the central and binding relation in his novels is that between ethics and affect, or, in a more informal translation, between behaving well and being emotionally open.

This relation is not unique to Dickens, but recurs in different forms throughout Victorian literature. George Eliot, for instance, posits just such a relation when she writes: "There is no general doctrine which is not capable of eating out our morality if unchecked by the deep-seated habit of direct fellow feeling with individual fellow men." Eliot's warning – contained in the stories of Bulstrode and Lydgate in *Middlemarch* – is against the grand schemes that ignore the one-to-one connection between human beings, and so stifle the necessary outgrowth of that connection, sympathy.

Prior to *Middlemarch*, another – perhaps the most moving – version of the Victorian advocacy of feeling is in that greatest of all Victorian poems, Tennyson's *In Memoriam*, where the struggle, again, is with a mass model, in this case emerging from geology: the evolution and extinction of whole species and its implication for humanity. Against this model, seeking some assurance of the significance of the individual life, Tennyson, for whom the question is made pressing by the death of his dearest friend, similarly finds his answer – finds, that is, the irreducible value of the single individual – in the strength of feeling of which that individual is capable: "And like a man in wrath the heart/Stood up and answer'd, 'I have felt'", an assertion no sooner made than brilliantly corrected: "No, like a child in doubt and fear". The amendment, displacing thundering certainty with a more tentative and ephemeral hope, is all the more persuasive for so doing.

In *Hard Times*, the threat is, as it is for Tennyson, the threat of numbers, though arising from another source. "My satire," Dickens wrote to Charles Knight in December 1854, "is against those who see figures and averages, and nothing else." Again and again he sets this binary before the reader, between statistics and the single individual, as in Sissy's account of her lessons with Mr M'Choakumchild:

And he said, This schoolroom is an immense

town, and in it there are a million of inhabitants,
and only five-and-twenty are starved to death in
the streets, in the course of a year. What is your
remark on that proportion? And my remark was
– for I couldn't think of a better one – that I
thought it must be just as hard upon those who
were starved, whether the others were a million,
or a million million. (I, ix)

Sissy is quickly recognisable as the novel's moral centre; in particular, as the counterpoint and foil to Louisa, to whom this conversation is relayed. From the outset, Sissy exemplifies that ordinary humanity that resists the Utilitarian system and repairs its damages.

Such damage is especially manifest in the novel's central female character. For despite its title, "the Condition of England" (Carlyle's tag for the privation of the urban working classes) is only part of the subject of *Hard Times*. Dickens's main attack is in his portrayal of the consequences of Utilitarian thought for his complex heroine, Louisa Gradgrind. In the moral vacuum at the core of the Utilitarian scheme, he places his test subject, a young woman, whose factual education and loveless marriage are both undertaken in strict adherence to its principles.

As she considers Bounderby's proposal of marriage, her father urges Louisa to set aside any question of love, and, instead, "to take into account

Jeremy Bentham's preserved skeleton, with a wax head on top, is dressed in his usual clothes and sitting on his favourite chair inside a wooden cabinet, as he decreed in his will. The cabinet is on display at University College London

the statistics of marriage, so far as they have yet been obtained, in England and Wales"; statistics that show "that a large proportion of these marriages are contracted between parties of very unequal ages" (I, xv). She is not yet 20, Bounderby, over 50. Taught to stifle natural feeling from her earliest childhood onwards, Louisa is left – or nearly so – with no moral compass, and in so being is brought to the brink of suicide or its dreaded alternative, prostitution (as the kept mistress of

James Harthouse). Her propulsion towards self-destruction, directly the consequence of her father's "system", is narrowly averted at the climax of the story:

> *...she cried out in a terrible voice, 'I shall die if you hold me! Let me fall upon the ground!' And he laid her down there and saw the pride of his heart and the triumph of his system, lying, an insensible heap, at his feet. (II, xii)*

Thomas Gradgrind himself is a misguided idealist, genuinely committed to that system which he judges best enables the progress of humanity and, more immediately, the welfare of his own children. Dickens models his character, as F.R. Leavis sees it, on Bentham's life-long friend and collaborator, James Mill (1773-1836). Mill's own son, the great Victorian philosopher, John Stuart Mill, was to describe many years later an education much like Louisa's, leading to a similar state of nervous collapse, from which he eventually emerged with a new appreciation for poetry and music. John Stuart Mill's autobiography was not published till 1873, but his education and subsequent depression, both taking place well before *Hard Times* was written, strangely furnish a real-life parallel for Louisa's story.

From the outset, Dickens uses the language of mutilation to describe the effects of Gradgrind's system: seeking to kill "the robber Fancy lurking within", it manages at least to "maim him and distort him!" (I, ii). Louisa is its worst casualty, because of her moral and intellectual stature, but its two other products – Gradgrind's son, Tom, and his school's star student, Bitzer – are equally, though differently, crippled by it. Tom becomes "that not unprecedented triumph of calculation which is usually at work on number one", manipulating his sister's affections to further his own plans for financial gain, and turning at last to crime (I, ix). Bitzer, whose stunted emotional development is exactly proportionate to his prowess as a Utilitarian scholar, is similarly incapable of acting in anyone's interests but his own.

"Twenty times," G.K. Chesterton wrote, "we have taken Dickens's hand and it has been sometimes hot with revelry and sometimes weak with weariness; but this time we start a little, for it is inhumanly cold; and then we realise that we have touched his gauntlet of steel." *Hard Times* leaves its reader with a sense of the permanent and lasting damage caused by a rigid commitment to Utilitarian principles. Although Dickens is at pains throughout to advocate an alternative education and outlook (one that will address itself "to the cultivation of the sentiments and affections"), no movement of plot or development of character takes place in the direction of this alternative. The worst of the novel's characters carry on nearly unchecked. Bitzer rises up the ladder in Bounderby's employment; Bounderby himself, although he is finally "to die of a fit in the Coketown street", remains till that time prosperous and more or less unchecked. Gradgrind changes, certainly, but becomes, in his changed state, altogether ineffectual, "much despised by his late political associates" (III, ix). And nothing mitigates the bleakness of Louisa's fate, her purpose, her happiness, and her intellectual confidence all destroyed, and so too, finally, her one hope, that of seeing her brother again.

The reintegration of the isolated individual into the society from which he or she has become alienated is central to the endeavour of the Victorian realist novel. Hence the importance of the happy ending in Victorian fiction, especially in the form of a marriage, which stands, simultaneously, for the gaining of personal fulfilment and social value. In *Hard Times*, the condition of alienation is so widespread that that endeavour is no longer practicable. The novel's two main characters remain marginalised, and the short paragraph on Sissy's ultimate attainment of domestic bliss hardly compensates, especially since no romance has preceded it. (Among Dickens's working plans, we find the following emphatic note: "Lover for Sissy? No. Decide on no love at all.") *Hard Times* states its case so forcefully that a comforting resolution – even a fictional one – is rendered impossible.

Is *Hard Times* socialist?

Undoubtedly many of Dickens's contemporaries saw *Hard Times* in that light. In a journal entry (12 August, 1854), Thomas Babington Macauley famously dismissed it as "sullen socialism"; the journalist John Hollingshead used the phrase "impracticable socialism" in a review. Indeed, Dickens's sustained depiction and indictment of the condition of the industrial poor in *Hard Times*, together with his demand for equal laws and more equitable living standards for rich and poor, made the perception widespread. Karl Marx himself, in an article in the New York Daily Tribune (1 August, 1854), included Dickens in "[t]he present splendid brotherhood of fiction-writers in England, whose graphic and eloquent pages have issued to the world more political and social truths than have been uttered by all the professional politicians, publicists and moralists put together".

As early as 1839, Dickens had visited the Manchester factories, and had declared in a letter to Edward FitzGerald (29 December, 1839): "what I have seen has disgusted and astonished me beyond all measure. I mean to strike the heaviest blow in my power for these unfortunate creatures." Some years later, in January 1854, as preparation for the writing of *Hard Times*, he went to Preston in Lancashire, during the cotton workers' strike, already in its sixth month at the time of this visit. In the novel, his sympathetic view of the unionised workers, undoubtedly informed by these visits, is manifest:

That every man felt his condition to be, somehow or other, worse than it might be; that every man considered it incumbent on him to join the set,

THE GREAT REFORM ACT AND THE CHARTIST MOVEMENT

In 1832, in the teeth of Tory opposition, a bill for sweeping parliamentary reform was passed, driven by the Whig Prime Minster, Charles Grey, 2nd Earl Grey (1764-1845; Prime Minister 1830-34). The Representation of the People Act 1832, which came to be known more informally as the First Reform Act or the Great Reform Act, brought about thoroughgoing changes to the nature and constitution of the electorate of England and Wales (similar legislation was enacted separately, around the same time, in Scotland and Ireland).

Among these changes was the enfranchisement of all male heads of households worth £10 or more, the creation of new constituencies in the large industrial cities – till then severely under-represented – and the abolition of "rotten"

towards the making of it better; that every man felt
his only hope to be in his allying himself to the
comrades by whom he was surrounded; and that in
this belief, right or wrong (unhappily wrong then),
the whole of that crowd were gravely, deeply,
faithfully in earnest; must have been as plain to any
one who chose to see what was there... (II, iv)

Notwithstanding this sympathy, however, and
despite the opinion of so many of Dickens's
contemporaries, *Hard Times* is emphatically not
socialist. The value judgement contained in the
narrator's parenthetical comment ("unhappily

or "pocket" boroughs. (These were small boroughs, with a number of representatives disproportionate to their size, in the hands of a single wealthy patron who controlled the votes. Gatton in Surrey, which had seven voters and returned two MPs to the House of Commons, was only one among several such examples.) In effect, political agency was shifted away from a narrow, landed, upper class to a much broader middle class, stretching down from wealthy traders and factory owners, to shopkeepers, small landowners, and tenant farmers. Nearly one in five men in England and Wales was enfranchised as a result of the Act, thus nearly doubling the size of the electorate.

What was radical change to some, however, to others did not go far enough: working men, the majority of one half of the population, remained disenfranchised. In the wake of the perceived failures of the first Reform Act, the London Working Men's Association was founded in 1836, in an effort more effectively to lobby for the rights of working men, by uniting men of all classes wrong then") indicates why. Quite simply, the novel's drive is not to promote but to avert mass action and the social upheaval that might ensue from such action.

Hard Times, or, to give it its full title in this context, *Hard Times for These Times*, belongs, recognisably, to a category of "industrial" novel, also called the "social problem" novel or "Condition of England" novel. Carlyle had coined the phrase "the Condition of England question" in his pamphlet, 'Chartism', to refer to the dispossession of the urban working classes and the growing disparity between rich and poor brought about by industrialisation. In direct response to his warning that "if something be not done, something will do itself one day, and in a fashion that will

committed to those rights.

In 1838, one of its founders, William Lovett (1800-1877), drew up a powerful manifesto: "The People's Charter: Being the Outline of An Act to provide for the Just Representation of the People of Great Britain and Ireland in the Commons' House of Parliament: Embracing the Principles of Universal Suffrage; No Property Qualification; Annual Parliaments; Equal Representation; Payment of Members; and Vote by Ballot". Hence was born the name and the movement, Chartism, the first working class movement in Britain, beginning in the more moderate political climate of London, but soon coming under the control of the radical political agitators of the north of England.

The Chartists presented three petitions listing their demands to Parliament, all of which were rejected: first in May 1839, then in May 1842, please nobody", a spate of novels appeared in the 1840s and 1850s that sought to alleviate the problem by rousing the sympathy of a middle-class readership for the condition of the industrial poor.

Hard Times is among these; other examples include Benjamin Disraeli's *Sybil* (1845); Elizabeth Gaskell's *Mary Barton* (1848) and *North and South* (1855); Charles Kingsley's *Alton Locke* (1850) and *Yeast* (1851). In the same time span, and in response to the same conditions, Friedrich Engels's seminal study, *The Condition of the Working Class in England* was published in 1844. *Hard Times*, like the other industrial fiction with which it is aligned, differs fundamentally from Engels's book, not so much in its perception of the problem, but in the solution that it proposes: a

and finally in April 1848. The rejection of the first two petitions, during the economic depression of the late 1830s and early 1840s – the "hungry forties", when thousands of working people died of starvation – set off strikes and riots across the country, the scale of protest generating a genuine fear, in the middle classes, about the possibility of a workers' revolution in Britain. The failure of the final petition, however, at a time of improved prosperity and economic growth, had little effect, and Chartism as a movement died away by 1850. Nonetheless, its legacy persisted well beyond its demise. Two further Reform Acts, in 1867 and 1884, brought about increasing representation for working men. Today, all but one of the Chartists' original six demands – the exception being the annual election of Parliament – have been implemented ■

solution that is unshakeably based in the individual, rather than in the mass.

Thus Dickens's sympathetic view of the workers' union in no way qualifies his conviction that their collectivist stance is delusional: "These men, through their very delusions, showed great qualities, susceptible of being turned to the happiest and best account" (II, iv). As the Marxist intellectual Raymond Williams observes in *Culture and Society* (1958): "His [Dickens's] positives do not lie in social improvement but rather in what he sees as the elements of human nature – personal kindness, sympathy, and forbearance. It is not the model factory against the satanic mill, nor is it the humanitarian experiment against selfish exploitation. It is, rather, individual persons against the System."

The topic of class – or more especially, Dickens's attitude to social aspiration – is more problematic. Williams points to an element of snobbery, quite apart from the indictment of particular economic or educational systems, in Dickens's portrayal of Bounderby.

A large part of the Victorian reader's feelings against Bounderby (and perhaps a not inconsiderable part of the twentieth-century intellectual's) rests on the... feeling that trade, as such, is gross. The very name (and Dickens uses his names with conscious and obvious effect), incorporating bounder, incorporates this typical feeling. The social criticism represented by bounder is, after all, a rather different matter from the question of aggressive economic individualism.

Peter Brooks, similarly, in *Realist Vision* (2005), finds the same kind of snobbery in Dickens's portrayal of Slackbridge, drawing attention particularly to the narrator's phrase for Slackbridge's clothing: "'mongrel dress' may be the real giveaway: Slackbridge is not a purebred English workingman, he slips dangerously through the nets of classification, like Bounderby he's snuck upwards on the social ladder". To Brooks, Dickens's representations, both of Blackpool and Slackbridge, expose his own middle-class anxieties: "For Dickens to turn Slackbridge into a sinister emblem of seduction and misrule... and to make part of Stephen's heroism his refusal to join the union... [is] of course a standard middle-class reaction of the time, and indeed well beyond Dickens's time."

The anxiety about unionisation might certainly be characterised as "middle-class", although we might also want to pause at so merely reductive a reading of Dickens's response to the threat of numbers. But the easy equation of this anxiety with the snobbery that frowns on social aspiration is more debatable, especially in the case of

Dickens, who himself achieved a considerable mobility within the innumerable gradations that make up the middle class – as the critic Fred Kaplan has put it, "many Victorians... from their superior class position, looked down on Dickens as a literary Bounderby". Dickens's target, in Bounderby and Slackbridge, as in countless other figures throughout his fiction, is not their movement up the social ladder, nor, primarily, their vulgarity, but their hypocrisy, discernible, in Slackbridge, in the power-mongering disguised as a concern for the common good. Gradgrind, by contrast, is redeemed by his sincerity and good-will, even when he holds to the system that Dickens repudiates.

In his essay on *Hard Times*, George Bernard Shaw also criticises Dickens's representation of Slackbridge and reads that representation in terms of class, calling it the "one real failure in the book... a mere figment of the middle-class imagination". But Shaw rightly associates the failure not so much with snobbery as with Dickens's rejection of unionisation. Slackbridge is the product of Dickens's distrust of numbers, of his firm commitment to the individual, rather than the collective, as the instrument for change. "I believe," he wrote in an article, 'On Strike', shortly after his visit to Preston, "that into the relations between employers and employed, as into all the relations of this life, there must enter something of feeling and sentiment; something of mutual explanation, forbearance, and consideration." Between such a proposition and the rallying cry on which *The Communist Manifesto* closes – "Working men of all countries, unite!" – the gap is unbridgeable.

How do we cope with Dickens's sentimentality?

Dickens's sentimentality raised for his first readers, and still raises, the same question that modern-day tearjerkers do in the cinema or on television: how should we feel about the kind of scene or situation designed to produce tears in its audience? Should we be embarrassed or ashamed by our own tearful responses? Is this cheap or vulgar emotion, with a "feel-good" quality to it, or even more uncomfortably, a voyeuristic quality, a pleasure taken in second-hand emotion?

The worldly-wise, knowing stance on such responses and the scenes that produce them is disgust or mockery. Oscar Wilde's famous comment on the most celebrated of Dickens's sentimental descriptions, the death of little Nell in *The Old Curiosity Shop* (1840-41), takes just this stance: "One must have a heart of stone to read the death of little Nell without laughing."

The witticism, seductive in its cynical knowingness as is so much of Wilde's wit, is not, on that account, necessarily true. Nowadays, there is increasing and welcome recognition of the importance of sentiment in stimulating ethical thought or behaviour, and new arguments, on this basis, for dissociating the words "sentiment" and "sentimental" from their condescending or pejorative overtones. In a powerful recent book, *In Defense of Sentimentality* (2004), the philosopher Robert Solomon tackles the fact that in many circles "sentimentality is one of those offenses against which there is no defence. For hardheaded activists as for intellectuals in general, 'sentimentality' is a dirty word, indicating bad taste, a paucity of arguments, sniveling morals, and an absence of backbone." Solomon argues compellingly that a different case needs to be made:

I take sentimentality to be nothing more nor less than the "appeal to tender feelings," and though one can manipulate and abuse such feelings (including one's own), and though they can on occasion be misdirected or excessive, there is nothing wrong with them as such and nothing (in that respect) wrong with literature that provokes us, that moves us to abstract affection or weeping... Sentimentality... does not impede, but rather prepares and motivates, our reacting in "the real world". It is not an escape

Portrait of Charles Dickens (1812-1880)

from reality or responsibility but, quite to the contrary, provides the precondition for ethical engagement rather than being an obstacle to it.

This is – or should be – our handle on Dickens's sentimentality. Dickens fully recognised and attempted to develop, as far as he was able, the ethical possibility inherent in sentiment. His strategy is to portray feeling individuals, for whom he wishes us to feel. As his friend, John Foster, described it quite simply in a review of *Hard Times*, "no thesis can be argued in a novel; but by a warm appeal from one heart, to a hundred thousand hearts quite ready to respond".

The principal focus of Dickens's sentimental mode in *Hard Times* is Stephen Blackpool, and the mode is most fully deployed in the scenes of Stephen and Rachael. The adoring piety with which he regards her, her utter selflessness and devotion to him, her unshakeable moral rectitude, all these are delivered in the language of high sentiment.

As she looked at him, saying, "Stephen?" he went down on his knee before her, on the poor mean stairs,

VICTORIAN MANCHESTER

Coketown is often taken to be based on Manchester, which Dickens visited in 1839, although his portrayal is informed, too, by his visit to another northern industrial town, Preston, in Lancashire, a few months before he began to write *Hard Times*.

Dickens's hyperbole reflects his reaction to the poverty and squalor of the great manufacturing cities. The boom in trade and commerce brought wealth to a few at the expense of the many. Contemporary records show that living conditions were unsanitary, disease rife, and life expectancy short, at least for the poor. Working conditions were frequently dangerous, with no regard for the health or safety of the workers. Children, who were paid a fraction of the adult wage, were on that account employed in greater numbers in the factories; the very

and put an end of her shawl to his lips.
"Thou art an Angel. Bless thee! Bless thee!"
*   "I am, as I have told thee, Stephen, thy poor friend.*
Angels are not like me. Between them, and a
working woman fu' of faults, there is a deep gulf set.
My little sister is among them, but she is changed."
(I, xiii)

The pathos reaches its height when Stephen is brought out of the mine shaft, to die shortly afterwards:

For, now, the rope came in, tightened and strained to

youngest made to crawl under machinery, where they sometimes became trapped, and died.

   Two contemporaneous representations of Manchester might be juxtaposed with that of Dickens's industrial city. One is Friedrich Engels's damning indictment in *The Condition of the Working Class in England* (1845). Engels's work is non-fiction, but his impassioned descriptions are all the more harrowing for their being, at the same time, matter-of-fact:

   The cottages are old, dirty, and of the smallest sort, the streets uneven, fallen into ruts and in part without drains or pavement; masses of refuse, offal, and sickening filth lie among standing pools in all directions; the atmosphere is poisoned by the effluvia from these, and laden and darkened by the smoke of a dozen tall factory chimneys. A horde of ragged women and children swarm about here, as filthy as the swine that thrive upon the garbage heaps and in the puddles... The race that lives in these ruinous cottages, behind *its utmost as it appeared, and the men turned heavily, and the windlass complained. It was scarcely endurable to look at the rope, and think of its giving way. But, ring after ring was coiled upon the barrel of the windlass safely, the connecting chains appeared, and finally the bucket with the two men holding on at the sides – a sight to make the head swim, and oppress the heart – and tenderly supporting between them, slung and tied within, the figure of a poor, crushed, human creature.*

A low murmur of pity went round the throng, and the women wept aloud... (III, vi)

broken windows, mended with oilskin, sprung doors, and rotten door-posts, or in dark, wet cellars, in measureless filth and stench, in this atmosphere penned in as if with a purpose, this race must really have reached the lowest stage of humanity.

In *North and South* (1854-55), published hard on the heels of *Hard Times*, Elizabeth Gaskell, herself a Mancunian, barely shows her reader a glimpse of the squalor that Engels records. Milton, Gaskell's fictional Manchester, is certainly not pretty.

For several miles before they reached Milton, they saw a deep lead-coloured cloud hanging over the horizon in the direction in which it lay... Nearer to the town, the air had a faint taste and smell of smoke; perhaps, after all, more a loss of the fragrance of grass and herbage than any positive taste or smell. Quick they were whirled over long, straight, hopeless streets of regularly-built houses, all small and of

The rope, literal and metaphorical at the same time, by which Stephen, in his last moments, is finally reunited with his community, is typical of Dickens's use of metaphor, a topic to which I will return later. Here it heightens the extreme pathos of the ending of Stephen's life.

> *"Rachael, beloved lass! Don't let go my hand. We may walk together t'night, my dear!"*
>
> *"I will hold thy hand, and keep beside thee, Stephen, all the way."*
>
> *"Bless thee! Will soombody be pleased to cover my face!"*

brick. Here and there a great oblong many-windowed factory stood up, like a hen among her chickens, puffing out black 'unparliamentary' smoke, and sufficiently accounting for the cloud...

But Gaskell elicits, from this industrial city, the conditions that foster a sturdy independence of thought and spirit in working people and manufacturers alike. The factory workers have "an open fearless manner"; "they came rushing along, with bold, fearless faces, and loud laughs and jests". Gaskell's "hen" is a far cry from Dickens's "elephant". Her Milton – a Mill Town, certainly, but also named for a great English poet – acts as a corrective to Coketown, just as John Thornton, Gaskell's exemplary capitalist, is a corrective to Josiah Bounderby. Thornton's is a robust – though later qualified – defense of *laissez-faire* capitalism, and his vision of Gaskell's beloved city is idealised and poetic: "our good town... the necessities of which give birth to [a] grandeur of conception" ∎

In his important defence of Victorian sentimentality, *Sacred Tears* (1987), Fred Kaplan argues that Dickens's novels "contain effective dramatizations of the moral significance of death... attempting purposely to arouse his reader's moral sentiments, reminding them that the more emotionally sensitive they are to death the more morally attentive they will be to the values of life". Kaplan traces the sentimentality of Victorian fiction – including Dickens's – to the 18th-century doctrine of moral sentiments, expounded by philosophers such as Francis Hutcheson, the 3rd Earl of Shaftesbury, David Hume, and (ironically enough as far as Dickens is concerned), Adam Smith, and transmitted to Victorian writers through the contemporary literature that it permeates.

In the description of Stephen's death and in other descriptions elsewhere in his fiction of the untimely deaths of the innocent, Dickens's roots in the 18th-century literature of "sensibility" are clearly discernible. The cult of sensibility in literature arose towards the middle of the 18th century, as a challenge to the emphasis on reason. The literature associated with this movement, by writers such as Laurence Sterne, Oliver Goldsmith, William Cowper, William Collins and many others, celebrates our vulnerability to emotion, our instincts for compassion, our capacity to weep. In the recurrent figure of a "man of feeling", frequently given to tears, this literature undoes, too, the gender stereotype that makes emotion a feminine characteristic.

In his portrayal of Blackpool, Dickens is of course enacting the attitude he wishes his readers to adopt, undermining the statistical view by directing attention to the life and love of a single worker, neglected in any numerical analysis. The perspective he enforces is that which Louisa gains for the first time when she visits Stephen's house.

> *For the first time in her life Louisa had come into one of the dwellings of the Coketown Hands; for the first time in her life she was face to face with anything like individuality in connexion with them. She knew of their existence by hundreds and by thousands. She knew what results in work a given number of them would produce in a given space of time. She knew them in crowds passing to and from their nests, like ants or beetles. But she knew from her reading infinitely more of the ways of toiling insects than of these toiling men and women. (II, vi)*

Tangential, but not unrelated, to the statistical view of the toiling poor, is another of Dickens's targets in the story of Blackpool, the law on divorce. At the time, as Bounderby informs Stephen, divorces had to be obtained by the passing of a private Act of Parliament, an extremely expensive process for anyone wishing to be divorced, and so available only to the wealthy. The motive that drives the sentimental idealism of Dickens's account of Stephen and Rachael, then, is the hard reality of a society ridden with inequality. Stephen's response to Bounderby's information is grim: "th' supposed unpossibility o' ever getting unchained from one another, at any price, on any terms, brings blood upon this land, and brings many common married fok to battle, murder, and sudden death" (I, xi).

Here, as throughout *Hard Times*, sentiment is juxtaposed with sharp and pointed comment, sometimes in the form of satire, on the injustices laid upon Stephen and other victims of the utilitarian tragedy. This trenchancy emerges in the descriptions of Coketown whose very streets constitute "an unnatural family, shouldering, and trampling, and pressing one another to death" (I, x), or in Dickens's contempt for hypocrisy, shown, for instance, in the social aspirations of the "Gradgrind school":

> *They liked fine gentlemen; they pretended that they did not, but they did. They became exhausted in imitation of them; and they yaw-yawed in their speech like them; and they served out, with an enervated air, the little mouldy rations of political economy, on which they regaled their disciples. (II, ii)*

And perhaps the most devastating of all his

pronouncements on Bounderby, the "Bully of humility", is this short plain sentence early on in the novel: "There was a moral infection of clap-trap in him" (I, vii). To Dickens, the dismissal of sentiment as "humbug", which Bounderby does so readily, is the tell-tale indication of the worst kind of humbug – that of the self-server who cares as little for fact as he does for any thing or person other than himself. Bounderby's final exposure, when the mysterious Mrs Pegler is identified, is as the author of a fiction utterly at variance with the facts he claims so stridently to uphold.

Always in its content, then, and often in its mode, *Hard Times* celebrates sentiment and warns against under-valuing it. No doubt aspects of its sentimentality may be considered excessive, straining against the bounds of credibility. Already by the time it was published, the critical and intellectual dismissal of Dickens's sentimentality had begun to swell with its popular appeal, reaching a crescendo in the course of the second half of the 19th century. In the words of his contemporary, Anthony Trollope, in a thinly-veiled caricature of Dickens as "Mr Popular Sentiment" in the novel *The Warden* (1855), "Mr Sentiment is certainly a very powerful man, and perhaps not the less so that his good poor people are so very good; his hard rich people so very hard; and the genuinely honest so very honest." Trollope goes on to comment, with some bitterness:

The artist who paints for the million must use glaring colours, as no one knew better than Mr Sentiment... and the radical reform which has now swept over [certain] establishments has owed more to the twenty numbers of Mr Sentiment's novel, than to all the true complaints which have escaped from the public for the last half century.

More sympathetically than Trollope, we might share in this recognition that Dickens's sentimentality is at the service rather than at the expense of his more hard-headed awareness of social disease and human shortcomings.

Why is the novel so unsubtle?

In Aldous Huxley's *Point Counter Point* (1928), the author's alter ego, the character Philip Quarles, jots down the following definition in his notebook: "Novel of ideas. The character of each personage must be implied; as far as possible, in the ideas of which he is mouthpiece." And a little further on, "People who can reel off formulated notions aren't quite real, they're slightly monstrous."

These comments might be taken together as a useful summary description of *Hard Times* and its principal character, Thomas Gradgrind. The subordination of character to idea, necessarily at the expense of subtlety, is critical to the way in which *Hard Times* works; in this sense, it matches Huxley's definition of the novel of ideas. Nowhere else in Dickens's fiction is his interest in plot, his flair for characterisation, his eye for detail, so manifestly secondary to the enforcing of a clear moral lesson. *Hard Times* is first and foremost a polemical work. Dickens himself repeatedly calls it a "satire". Thomas Gradgrind – who has named two of his children Adam Smith and Malthus – is a mouthpiece for the ideas Dickens wishes to critique, and in so being, is rendered monstrous, almost physically so, in the narrator's description at the opening of the novel:

> *The emphasis was helped by the speaker's square wall of a forehead, which had his eyebrows for its base, while his eyes found commodious cellarage in two dark caves, overshadowed by the wall. The emphasis was helped by the speaker's mouth, which was wide, thin, and hard set. The emphasis was helped by the speaker's voice, which was inflexible, dry, and dictatorial. The emphasis was helped by the speaker's hair, which bristled on the skirts of his bald head, a plantation of firs to keep the wind from its shining surface, all covered with knobs, like the crust of a plum pie... (I, i)*

In this portrait, Dickens is drawing on the pseudo-science of phrenology – which linked physiognomy, especially the shape of the skull, to temperament or personality – to create a character whose very appearance is an aspect of his misguided beliefs. The grotesque or monstrous element in Gradgrind's physical appearance is all the more pronounced in Bitzer, more completely the creature of the Utilitarian system.

> *His cold eyes would hardly have been eyes, but for the short ends of lashes which, by bringing them into immediate contrast with something paler than themselves, expressed their form. His short-cropped hair might have been a mere continuation of the sandy freckles on his forehead and face. His skin was so unwholesomely deficient in the natural tinge, that he looked as though, if he were cut, he would bleed white. (I, ii)*

The contrast of Sissy with Bitzer, part of the extended metaphor of light and darkness that runs through the novel and represents a range of equivalent oppositions, such as true wisdom and ignorance, or moral sensitivity and moral insensibility, is, again, direct and unsubtle:

> *"whereas the girl was so dark-eyed and dark-haired, that she seemed to receive a deeper and more lustrous colour from the sun, when it shone*

upon her, the boy was so light-eyed and light-haired that the self-same rays appeared to draw out of him what little colour he ever possessed." (I, ii)

The contrast belongs to the clearly defined binary scheme that operates in *Hard Times*, and that escalates the novel of ideas to allegory.

In The Realistic Imagination (1981), George Levine notes the recurrence in Victorian literature of "that familiar [battle], most allegorically handled in *Hard Times*, between life, with all its emotion and vitality, and utilitarianism, with all its analytic calculation", going on to add: "The organic and the mechanical are opposed forces in Victorian fiction." As Levine suggests, Dickens's binary view, constructing an allegory of good and evil, and discernible not only in his other novels, but also in Victorian fiction more generally, is most obvious in *Hard Times*.

The novel's governing figure is that of antithesis, the dual components of which struggle against each other for mastery: in abstract form, as Fact and Fancy; in the form of alternative worlds, as Coketown and Sleary's Circus; in individual characters, as Sissy and Bitzer; in the warring elements of the human psyche, as head and heart. Dickens shows the struggle between the two parts of the antithesis as it operates in the world at large, and as it is played out, too, within his major characters, in particular, Louisa, where its resolution, after her crisis, is literalised in the laying of her head on Sissy's heart: "let me lay this head of mine upon a loving heart!' 'O lay it here!'" cried Sissy. 'Lay it here, my dear'" (III, i). In set pieces such as this last, furthermore, as in the declamatory style of so many of his characters' key speeches, Dickens's pronounced allegorical tendency is the more heavily accentuated by his manifest leaning to theatricality, and, in particular, by his inclination to melodrama.

The mode of allegory is highlighted, too, by Dickens's fondness for names that have a representative significance. Hence Gradgrind (from "grindstone", according to Dickens's working notes) and M'Choakumchild, the latter introduced to us in a chapter titled "Murdering the Innocents", to emphasise his role as a modern-day Herod. Bounderby, too, is completely a bounder, the name capturing both his heedless progress up the financial ladder and his obnoxious obtrusiveness.

The use of names to emphasise the personification of a ruling idea or personality trait is a practice Dickens derived from the comedies of the Renaissance playwright, Ben Jonson (1572-1637), whom he greatly admired. Dickens actually took an acting role, as the character Bobadill, in an 1845 revival of Jonson's *Every Man in his Humour* (1598), a play in which each character – some with names such as Knowell, Wellbred, and Brainworm

– illustrates the working of a dominant "humour" or temperament. Similarly, the characters of Jonson's *Bartholomew Fair* (1614), for instance, have names such as Littlewit, Quarlous and, most hilariously, Zeal-of-the-land Busy (this last being a hypocritical Puritan), with which Dickens's clearly resonate.

If the names of some key proponents convey something limited and one-dimensional about the Utilitarian view, so too does Dickens's use of metonymy in *Hard Times*. Metonymy is the figure of speech in which a part or attribute represents something directly related to it (as, for instance, "the Crown", or "the pen is mightier than the sword"). Usually a figure that connects or relates the part to the whole – the object to that which it represents – it produces in this novel the impression of separation or dissociation. This impression begins at the very outset, when Gradgrind is described as a collection of physical attributes (forefinger, forehead, eyes, mouth, voice, hair, head) rather than as a complete individual; soon afterwards, another set of separate metonymies constitutes Bitzer's definition of a horse. Further on, Mrs Sparsit is represented by her "Coriolanian style of nose and... dense black eyebrows" (I, vii); her deceased husband described as a headless torso ("a slender body, weakly supported on two long slim props, and surmounted by no head worth mentioning"). We also have the recurrent reduction of the power-loom workers to "Hands",

> *a race who would have found more favour with some people, if Providence had seen fit to make them only hands, or, like the lower creatures of the seashore, only hands and stomachs. (I, x)*

The common tag for factory workers acquires, in Dickens's use, a potent effect of dismemberment. Bounderby's metonymy of "turtle and venison and a gold spoon" – standing for an imaginary meal at which turtle soup and venison, both luxuries,

J. HILLIS MILLER ON DICKENS'S USE OF LANGUAGE

In a well-known essay, "The Fiction of Realism: Sketches by Boz, Oliver Twist, and Cruikshank's Illustrations" (1971), the leading Dickens scholar, J. Hillis Miller, sets out to scrutinise Dickens's characteristic use of the two figures of speech, metaphor and metonymy. Miller's point of departure is the influential distinction proposed by the linguist and literary theorist, Roman Jakobson – that metonymy, based on direct connection or nearness, represents that which it stands for, where metaphor, based on resemblance, displaces that which it stands for.

The connection in the first, between the figure and what it signifies, is direct and "real"; in the second, imaginative, "poetic" or unreal. (The metonymy, "the Crown", for instance, refers to an item actually worn by, would be eaten or served with a gold spoon, this meal itself being a metonymy for extravagance and opulence – which sets the "Hands" grasping in vain at a surreal assemblage of objects, accentuates the impression of dissociation and reduction. So too does the metonymy of Head and Heart, extending through the whole course of the novel, and made explicit by Gradgrind in the aftermath of Louisa's breakdown ("there is a wisdom of the Head, and… there is a wisdom of the Heart" (III, i)). The splitting of head and heart is at the expense of the whole individual, producing a vision that is fractured and distorted.

---

and thus directly associated with, the monarch, but when we call someone a "night owl" or a "bookworm", the metaphor is based on an imagined resemblance, rather than a direct or real connection. Syntactically and imaginatively, in the statements, "he's a night owl", or "she's a bookworm", the owl or the worm becomes – substitutes for, displaces – the person described.)

Jakobson contends that the tendency of realist fiction is to metonymy; of the poetic text, to metaphor. In his essay, Miller queries this demarcation of metonymy and metaphor. Dickens's metonymy, he claims, as exemplified in his *Sketches by Boz* – as he sees it, "a characteristic expression of Dickens's genius… contain[ing] all of Dickens's later work in embryo" – has the fictive quality of metaphor, so that the text itself is less a literal description of real things, than a self-enclosed literary construction, a pure fiction. Using as examples of metonymy, objects from the *Sketches* that are similar to Stone Lodge and the brass door-knob, he argues, on their basis, that "metonymy is as much a fiction as

Dickens's metonymy in *Hard Times* most characteristically takes the form of body parts, to show a society that is, in the fullest sense, unwholesome, its members taken apart by a pure materiality. In this form, metonymy also falls into the sub-category of synecdoche, where the figure is actually – that is, physically and literally – a part of that which it represents, rather than simply related to it ('greybeard' and "wheels" are common examples). Dickens's "Hands", "Heart", "Head", all synecdoches, make the impression of dissociation, or the severance of part from whole, the more pronounced.

The converse type of synecdoche, in which the whole represents the part (as in 'England beat Argentina', where 'England' and 'Argentina' refer

metaphor. Both are the assertion of a false identity or a false causal connection... A man's door-knocker is no necessary indication of his personality. It only seems so to the imagining mind."

Miller concludes that to read any text as referring to anything out of itself is always erroneous. "Any literary text is both self-referential and extra-referential, or rather it is open to being not seen as the former and mistakenly taken as the latter."

Nor does he stop here. "All language," he goes on, "is figurative, displaced."

As readers, whether we accept or dispute this conclusion, we might in any case question the adequacy of a generalisation about "all language" to the particular and special qualities of Dickens's (and other authors') writing. And indeed, despite his own generalisations, it is exactly these qualities that emerge in Miller's analysis, in the important insight that Dickens's figuration collapses to football teams, not the entire country), is similarly dissociative in *Hard Times*. In the world of the novel, the whole does not stand for the individual parts, the single human being is detached from the larger impersonal collectives, such as the union, or the mass of humanity on which statistical computation is based. And lastly, by a reverse process, inanimate objects mutate to synechdoches and a connection is established where none should exist, so that Gradgrind's house, "Stone Lodge", and Bounderby's "brazen" door-plate and door-knob, bearing the attributes of their hardened and unfeeling owners, seem literally to become a part of them.

Inevitably, these elements of Dickens's style in *Hard Times* add up to hyperbole. Such

the demarcation of metonymy and metaphor.

Certainly where *Hard Times* is concerned, the instability of the distinction between metaphor and metonymy, and the flouting by both figures of their conventional func-tions, are incontrovertible. Metaphor – such as the rope by which Stephen Blaćkpool is pulled out of the pit – often has a literal aspect; equally, objects such as Gradgrind's house and Bounderby's door-knob, which Miller might categorise as metaphor, work in the text as synechdoches, here over-stepping imaginary resemblance to make an unnatural connection.

Just as frequently, metonymy skirts the functions both of literal representation and imaginative association, producing instead an effect of separation or splitting, the effect that characterises a world – not literary rather than real, but both real and literary at once – devoid of coherence or meaning ■

exaggeration is the necessary constituent of his polemical purpose, and critical to the rhetorical strategy that he employs. At the same time, we should recognise, too, that the hyperbole belongs not to a current reality, but a projected future, a dystopia, in which Utilitarian thought is allowed to develop without check or mitigation. The society that might be produced by such a culmination is, as Dickens perceives it, distorted and grotesque. One anonymous reviewer in the Westminster Review complained explicitly of this distortion, or, in his words, "compression and disfigurement":

> One can have no more pleasure in being present at this compression and disfigurement... nor in following these poor souls, thus intellectually halt and maimed, through life, than in seeing Chinese ladies hobbling through a race.

The complaint exactly answers Dickens's purpose. The strong sense of the grotesque impressed upon his reader – by the peculiar physical characteristics of his characters, their odd names, their reduction to dissociated inanimate body parts – conveys his vision of a world driven by the theories against which he bears arms. This is the deformation that the narrator predicts in his rhetorical question at the beginning of the novel: "...dost thou think that thou wilt always kill outright the robber Fancy lurking within – or sometimes only maim him and

Gradgrind (Patrick Allen) and Bounderby (Timothy West) enjoying a ride at the circus in ITV's 1977 TV adaptation

distort him!" (I, ii). The question, with its allusion to the story of Ali Baba and the Forty Thieves, creates in us an instant, unexpected sympathy for the thieves' torment as Morgiana pours hot oil upon them, just the response that Dickens demands to the disabling consequences of a utilitarian education.

TEN FACTS ABOUT
Hard Times

1.
Hard Times, at 117,400 words, is the shortest of Dickens's novels, and much shorter than the two previous Dickens novels which were serialised: *The Old Curiosity Shop* (227,500 words) and *Barnaby Rudge* (263,650 words),

2.
The circulation of Household Words, the periodical Dickens launched in 1850, rose to about 30,000 but was slipping by the time he wrote *Hard Times*. Pressed by his printers to do something about this, he decided to serialise the novel in its pages. The ploy succeeded. The first extract appeared in April 1854 and circulation doubled within ten weeks.

3.
Hard Times is the only Dickens novel not to have scenes set in London.

4.
The novelist knew Westminster well, having been a parliamentary reporter in his early twenties. But he had no desire to be an MP and in the year *Hard Times* was published he described Westminster as

"miserably imbecilic". In the novel itself Westminster is referred to as the "great cinder heap in London".

5.

George Orwell praised *Hard Times* for its "generous anger" but castigated Dickens for being confused politically. There is, he said, an "utter lack of any constructive suggestion anywhere in his work. He attacks the law, parliamentary government, the educational system and so forth, without ever clearly suggesting what he would put in their places". Others, such as the Marxist critic Raymond Williams, have echoed Orwell's criticism.

6.

Hard Times was made into a silent film in 1915, and has been adapted twice as a mini-series for television, first in 1977 and secondly in 1994, with Bob Peck as Gradgrind and Alan Bates as Bounderby.

7.

The great art critic John Ruskin frequently referred to Dickens 's works, declaring that he knew *Pickwick Papers* almost "by heart"., and sending at least one of his own autographed books to Dickens as a gift. *Hard Times* was his favourite

Dickens novel. He approved of its denunciation of selfishness and the corrupting power of money.

8.

No novel of Dickens's is more topical than *Hard Times*. If you'd asked a reader in 1854 what it was about you'd have received a three-word answer – "The Preston Strike". The strike, involving 20,000 workers in Preston's cotton mills, ran from October 1853 to May 1854. The novel was serialised in (in 5,000-word instalments the author found tricky) from 1 April to 12 August, 1854.

9.

Two principal organisers led the strikers' fight for better wages, George Cowell and Mortimer Grimshaw. Both Lancashire men, they were veteran "Chartists", and textile workers. Cowell was the more reasonable of the two. Grimshaw ("the Lancashire thunderer") was seen by many as a demagogue and rabble rouser. Dickens heard Grimshaw speak when he visited Preston to report on the strike – and disliked him. Another radical, Ernest Jones, came up from London, to mobilise the strikers (as does Slackbridge in the novel). After eight weary months, the strikers surrendered. Cowell and Grimshaw were charged with conspiracy, but the charges were later dropped.

10.

Dickens's Household Words was not partisan. A few months after *Hard Times* concluded its run, his magazine serialised another novel about working conditions in the mills, Elizabeth Gaskell's *North and South*. Mrs Gaskell's novel is notably more sympathetic towards mill owners than *Hard Times*.

The circus, as depicted in ITV's 1977 adaptation of Hard Times

Is *Hard Times* a realist novel?

The question of what might or might not constitute realism has a long and continuing debate behind it, and it is not a question that *Hard Times* can settle. In Dickens's own time, George Henry Lewes, who, in 1855, inaugurated the use of the term in English literary criticism, summarises the nature and limits of Dickens's realism as follows:

> Unreal and impossible as these types [Dickens's characters] were, speaking a language never

POLITICAL GRADGRINDERY

The *Oxford English Dictionary* glosses the word "Gradgrind" as "A person who is hard and cold, and solely interested in facts", listing usages dating from 1855; the derivatives "Gradgrinding" and "Gradgrindery" are also listed. Within a year of the publication of *Hard Times*, then, Dickens's name for his central character had passed into the English language. Today, it is very much part of common parlance in the English-speaking world.

Notably, for instance, it was repeatedly deployed in the criticisms made of Michael Gove's educational reforms. In The Guardian on 21 January, 2011, for example, Stephen Bates compared Gradgrind's opening words in *Hard Times* – "Now, what I want is, Facts. Teach these boys and girls nothing but heard in life... these unreal figures affected the uncritical reader with the force of reality; and they did so in virtue of their embodiment of some real characteristic vividly presented.

Interestingly, the touch of reality, in Lewes's perception, heightens rather than mitigates the impossible nature of Dickens's representations. Lewes was the long-term companion of George Eliot, and in the view of many modern commentators, such as Philip Davis in his literary history, *The Victorians* (2002), the "high realism" of the later Victorian period, of which Eliot is so powerful an exemplar, is to some extent a

Facts. Facts alone are wanted in life" – with Gove's plans for the national curriculum as described by him on the *Today* programme the day before: "I just think there should be facts... I am saying we need to have facts in the curriculum – facts, knowledge."

The National Union of Teachers denounced "Gradgrind Gove's pub quiz curriculum" at their annual conference in 2013, while, in The New Statesman, the then Education Secretary himself accused those resistant to his proposals of mischaracterising them as "the rule of Gradgrind".

Gove is not the first politician who has been associated with Gradgrind. In June, 2010, Philip Hensher in The Independent called the MP and former government minister, Chris Bryant, a "Gradgrind" because of his reference to "useless modern foreign languages such as French". And in The Daily Telegraph the following year (26 December, 2011), Philip Johnston referred to Gordon Brown as "Gordon Gradgrind", for being "a personification of puritanical gloom" ∎

"corrective reaction against the work of Dickens".

In the present day, the parameters – and in some fundamental respects, the terms – of the discussion have altered significantly. At least where its subject matter is concerned, *Hard Times* certainly answers to the long-standing association, especially celebrated in the writings of the Marxist philosopher and critic, Georg Lukács, of realism with the depiction of unjust or unequal social conditions and the exposure, especially, of the plight of the poor. But for scholars such as Fred Kaplan, as for Lewes and other of Dickens's contemporaries, Dickens's sentimentality, especially in such depictions, is at the expense of the "realistic" qualities of his fiction. To Kaplan, however, this is precisely the point:

> Victorian sentimentality should not be evaluated in the terms offered by the mimetic tradition in both literature and the general culture, to which it is in fundamental, purposeful opposition.

Sentimental fiction creates the world that ought to be, rather than simply imitating the world that is. Dickens in particular,

> throughout is basically non-mimetic. His main interest is not in accurately representing society but in creating a social world within his fiction that accurately embodies the moral paradigms

that he believes are innate within human nature.

J. Hillis Miller, too, argues, on somewhat different grounds, the non-mimetic character of Dickens's fiction. To Miller, what functions in Dickens's narrative as metonymy (clothes, furniture, houses, standing for the persons to whom they belong), giving us the illusion of mimesis – of a solid connection to the real entity that it represents – is as fictitious as metaphor, since there is no real or necessary connection between a man and his house, or his door-knob. More broadly, if realism is to do with the representation of an outside world, then the pronouncedly metaphorical quality of Dickens's (and others') text makes it non-representational. Because the connections made by metaphor are imaginary and literary, rather than "real" (in the sense that there is no actual resemblance between a courageous fighter and a lion, or an avid reader and a worm which feeds on books, no matter how vivid the comparisons might be), it follows for Miller that the text of Dickens's novel, characteristically metaphorical, should be understood on that basis – on the basis, that is, of its metaphorical quality – not as pointing outwards, to an external "reality", but as an enclosed, self-referential fiction.

Other critics have pointed to Dickens's theatricality. Among them, John Glavin in his essay, "Dickens and Theatre" in the *Cambridge Companion To Charles Dickens* (2001), declares:

> Pretty much everyone agrees Dickens's fiction is spectacular. I'm going to literalize that claim to say that in an era of Spectacular Theatre Dickens wrote a comparably Spectacular fiction, where Spectacular, on both stage and page meant something like realism eradicated.

Subsequently, in his book *Realist Vision*, the Yale academic, Peter Brooks, tackling the issue specifically in relation to *Hard Times,* has expressed a position that is a combination of Miller's and Kaplan's. Brooks suggests that the non-mimetic quality of *Hard Times* – its pronouncedly "literary" elements, such as those I have listed in the preceding section – is itself part of a narrative strategy that matches the subject of the novel. Dickens's critique of factuality is heightened by a narrative that rejects factuality in its deliberate recourse to poeticising, idealisation, excess.

In other words, the refusal to render Coketown literally is itself an aspect of the indictment of the empire of fact that Coketown embodies. Brooks does not deny Miller's characterisation of Dickens's text as non-mimetic or non-representational; on the contrary, he endorses it, but, by arguing that this is deliberate and strategic on Dickens's part, he does implicitly, and rightly, reject what Miller implicitly suggests: that Dickens's text in some respect imposes upon us – that it is, so to speak, in bad faith.

To Brooks, representation itself, or more particularly, "the mendacities of systems of representation", is the subject of *Hard Times*. Thus he finds in the opening scene in the schoolroom a critique of realistic representation, as exemplified in Bitzer's definition of a horse – "Quadruped. Gramnivorous. Forty teeth" and so on – and in the subsequent pronouncements by the Utilitarian educators on interior decoration:

"You are not to have, in any object of use or ornament, what would be a contradiction in fact. You don't walk upon flowers in fact; you cannot be allowed to walk upon flowers in carpets. You don't find that foreign birds and butterflies come and perch upon your crockery; you cannot be permitted to paint foreign birds and butterflies upon your crockery. You never meet with quadrupeds going up and down walls; you must not have quadrupeds represented upon walls. You must use," said the gentleman, "for all these purposes, combination and modifications (in primary colours) of mathematical figures which are susceptible of proof and demonstration. This is the new discovery. This is fact. This is taste." (I, ii)

As a deliberate counter to this version of realistic representation, the narrator's practice is what Brooks calls "non-representation", citing, as an instance, the following famous description of Coketown:

> *It was a town of red brick, or of brick that would have been red if the smoke and ashes had allowed it; but as matters stood it was a town of unnatural red and black like the painted face of a savage. It was a town of machinery and tall chimneys, out of which interminable serpents of smoke trailed themselves for ever and ever and never got uncoiled. It had a black canal in it, and a river that ran purple with ill-smelling dye, and vast piles of building full of windows where there was a rattling and a trembling all day long, and where the piston of the steam-engine worked monotonously up and down like the head of an elephant in a state of melancholy madness. (I, v)*

This account, as a number of commentators have observed, offers, instead of a realistic portrayal of an industrial town, a highly charged and imaginative rendering of it. The conversion of the piston of the steam engine to the elephant head is an instance of Miller's equation of metonymy with metaphor. More generally, the condition of alienation, so endemic to Coketown, is conveyed by the metamorphosis of an English industrial town into a hostile foreign territory, with its painted savage, its serpents, its mad elephant. The self-referentiality that Miller posits is confirmed by the closing scenes of the novel, where, in retrospect, we recognise the black face of Tom Gradgrind, literally "the painted face of a savage" – which, though a disguise, is in fact the badge of his criminality – as having already been prefigured in the description given here. In fact another critic, Paul Schlicke, in his study of the circus in *Hard Times*, argues that the details of the savage, the serpents, and the elephant in the description of Coketown, all add up to a kind of monstrous version of the circus, its monstrosity pertaining to repression: the repression of Fancy, and the virtues associated with Fancy, in Coketown.

Yet we might stop short, nonetheless, of denying a commitment to the "real" in such a representation. Exactly what *Hard Times* insists upon, with some vehemence, is that "reality" is not to be identified with "fact". The point made by Bitzer's metonymical definition is precisely that it does not render its subject, the horse, realistically; conversely, the narrator's description of Coketown, by the novel's own criteria, does. The critique of fact demands that we relocate reality outside the realm of fact, in that everyday human experience that is not reducible to the purely factual.

In upholding the primacy of experience, *Hard Times* shows its common purpose with other more recognisably realist texts. In this respect, George Levine's comments on George Eliot in *The Realistic Imagination* might also be made of Dickens. Her narrative, says Levine, conveys "the impression of an empirically shareable experience. Its relation to reality may be mediated by consciousness, but it is authenticated by the appeal of consciousness to the shared consciousness of a community of readers." Extending this claim from Eliot to Dickens, we might observe that the fanciful or literary quality of the text of *Hard Times* is authenticated – granted a reality – because it assumes, and appeals to, a shared perception. The world it describes is not circumscribed by the singular view of its author or narrator, but is manifest to the larger "community of readers". Dickens wants us all to see Coketown as he does, just as Sissy's desire to have flowers on her wallpaper represents a more widespread human proclivity.

Critical to the project of the realist text, moreover, is not merely authenticity of representation, but also – through the faithful rendering of a world – the denial of the isolation of the individual. By directing the attention outwards, away from the self, the realist narrative urgently presses the relation between individuals, between self and other, or many others. Putting aside the critical niceties, we can readily list those aspects of

Hard Times that militate against what a general reader might understand by realism, namely, a truthful or realistic representation of individuals and the world they live in. The novel, as we have seen, exaggerates, idealises, sentimentalises. But it also does this:

> *She was very cleanly and plainly dressed, had country mud upon her shoes and was newly come from a journey. The flutter of her manner, in the unwonted noise of the streets; the spare shawl, carried unfolded on her arm; the heavy umbrella, and little basket; the loose long-fingered gloves, to which her hands were unused; all bespoke an old woman from the country, in her plain holiday clothes, come into Coketown on an expedition of rare occurrence. (I, xii)*

This kind of description – here introducing Mrs Pegler, who is later discovered to be Bounderby's mother – is characteristic of the realist narrative, the narrative, that is, of ordinary people in ordinary situations. Its detail not only creates a clearer picture of the subject represented but also works to another end, from which such clarity cannot be decoupled. The focus on the ordinary is necessarily impelled by an ethical purpose. In this particular instance, as elsewhere in the realist fiction of the Victorian era, the minute details of dress and manner, all conducing to an impression of the accuracy of the representation, also invite the reader's engagement with the old lady's cleanliness and simplicity, her nervousness, the spareness of her shawl, the heaviness of her umbrella. The attention given to the ordinary in this passage is a moral attention.

The realist narrative's interest in ordinary humanity emerges, moreover, not only in its detailed descriptions of people, but also of their surroundings. Here is Coketown on a hot summer's day:

> Sun-blinds, and sprinklings of water, a little cooled the main streets and the shops; but the mills, and the courts and alleys, baked at a fierce heat. Down upon the river that was black and thick with dye, some Coketown boys who were at large – a rare sight there – rowed a crazy boat, which made a spumous track upon the water as it jogged along, while every dip of an oar stirred up vile smells. (II, i)

A picture such as this conveys the everyday world that human beings inhabit, and their everyday experience in that world. The reader's focus is shifted temporarily from the main characters of the book to the other inhabitants of the town. The anonymous "boys" in the picture are brought fleetingly to life: their unaccustomed liberty, the discrepancy between their boyish pleasure in rowing and the pollution against which it contends. The adjective "crazy" is laden with meaning.

In her book, *The Sovereignty of Good* (1970), the philosopher and novelist Iris Murdoch adopts the word "attention" to express "the idea of a just and loving gaze directed upon an individual reality", and she identifies this kind of attention as "the characteristic and proper mark of the active moral agent". The qualifier "individual" is critical: "attention" signifies a moral relation whose locus is the individual, a relation between the individual self and individual others. In Dickens's fiction, this quality of attention is frequently, though not only or always, achieved in its detail. Take this account of the appearance of Stephen Blackpool, speaking with Mr Bounderby about his wish for a divorce.

In another moment, he stood as he had stood all the time – his usual stoop upon him; his pondering face addressed to Mr Bounderby, with a curious expression on it, half shrewd, half perplexed, as if his mind were set upon unravelling something very difficult; his hat held tight in his left hand, which rested on his hip; his right arm, with a rugged propriety and force of action, very earnestly emphasising what he said: not least so when it always paused, a little bent, but not withdrawn, as he paused. (I, xi)

The carefully listed details of expression and

gesture attest to the just and loving gaze turned upon Stephen. By looking in this way, the narrator establishes a relation between himself (and by extension, the reader) and the subject of his gaze; this is the relation to which the realist narrative aspires, the relation which George Eliot calls, in a famous passage in *Adam Bede*, "the fibre of sympathy connecting me with that vulgar citizen who weighs out my sugar". The point of the realistic representation, in other words, is to bring about a meaningful relation between self and other: the relation shown to us in *Hard Times* not only by the narrator, but also by the just and loving perspectives of the novel's key moral characters, Rachael and Sissy.

As I see it, "relation" or "engagement" expresses the moral thrust of the realist vision, the object to which its detailed representation aspires. In Dickens's case, we might add, such representation can frequently be more just than loving. The tenor of his attention varies with his subject, ranging from compassion to outright condemnation. Here is his description of the demagogue, Slackbridge, for instance:

> *...the comparison between the orator and the crowd of attentive faces turned towards him, was extremely to his disadvantage... He was not so honest, he was not so manly, he was not so good-humoured; he substituted cunning for their simplicity, and passion*

for their safe solid sense. An ill-made, high-
shouldered man, with lowering brows, and his
features crushed into an habitually sour expression,
he contrasted most unfavourably, even in his
mongrel dress, with the great body of his hearers in
their plain working clothes. (II, iv)

The narrator denies sympathy to Slackbridge because it is incompatible with the fullness of his sympathy for Slackbridge's audience. It might be argued that the limit of Dickens's sympathy is also the limit of his realism, since all subjects are emphatically not equal to his view. In the harshest of his criticism, however, his attention and his engagement are still not in question. The reverse of the relational view is not the judgemental perspective of Dickens's narrator, but a quite different kind of gaze, also shown in the novel: the watchful but disengaged gaze of Mrs Sparsit. Mrs Sparsit is another instance of the solitary, dissociated individual who characterises the Utilitarian world; her ruling emotion, what we would now call schadenfreude, the perverse pleasure taken in the misfortune of others. The particular object of her gaze is Louisa, daily descending the metaphorical staircase she has constructed for her in her own mind.

Mrs Sparsit sat at her window all day long looking
at the customers coming in and out, watching the

postmen, keeping an eye on the general traffic in the
street, revolving many things in her mind, but above
all, keeping her attention on her staircase. (II, ix)

Her minute watchfulness, maintained till the end of the final encounter between Louisa and Harthouse, is the antithesis provided by the binary scheme of the novel to the stance of engaged attention. Its tendency is to the opposite extremes, of misunderstanding, hatred, and isolation.

It should be acknowledged, however, that if closely observed detail shows the realist attitude, this kind of detail in *Hard Times* – so vehemently polemical – is sparse in comparison to most of Dickens's novels. Nonetheless, to the extent that *Hard Times* sustains a compassionate focus on the ordinary, we might judge it to be a "realist" text, even as we register those aspects of the novel that render the ordinary extraordinary, and so strain against what we might, at the most informal level, understand by "realism". We might recognise, too, that in itself, the realist mode, which consists in minute and careful observation, and the sentimental, which paints broadly and in heightened colours, are not necessarily mutually exclusive. In this novel, realism and sentimentality coincide in the object to which they tend, the object of always resolving the mass of humanity into individuals, separately observed.

Where's the sex?

Towards the end of the chapter entitled "Mr Bounderby", in which we are first introduced to that redoubtable character, he looks in on the children's study and asks Louisa for a kiss.

> *"You can take one, Mr Bounderby," returned Louisa, when she had coldly paused, and slowly walked across the room, and ungraciously raised her cheek towards him, with her face turned away.*
>
> *"Always my pet, ain't you, Louisa?" said Mr Bounderby. "Good-bye, Louisa!"*
>
> *He went on his way, but she stood on the same spot, rubbing the cheek he had kissed, with her handkerchief, until it was burning red. She was still doing this, five minutes afterwards.*
>
> *"What are you about, Loo?" her brother sulkily remonstrated. "You'll rub a hole in your face."*
>
> *"You may cut the piece out with your penknife, if you like, Tom. I wouldn't cry!" (I, iv)*

The violence of Louisa's aversion to the kiss shows her awareness, already at the age she is then ("fifteen or sixteen"), that Bounderby's interest is sexual rather than purely paternal. A comparably violent reaction is shown by Louisa's precursor, the more mature Edith Dombey in Dickens's *Dombey and Son*, when Carker, with whom she later elopes, kisses her hand.

Edith did not withdraw the hand, nor did she strike his fair face with it, despite the flush upon her cheek, the bright light in her eyes, and the dilation of her whole form. But when she was alone in her own room, she struck it on the marble chimney-shelf, so that, at one blow, it was bruised, and bled; and held it from her, near the shining fire, as if she could have thrust it in and burned it.

Sexual desire – invariably manifested as male – is always problematic in Dickens's moral scheme, as in that of many of his contemporaries. The problem, roughly, is this: how to reconcile desire, which seeks sensory gratification from another, with the kind of selfless love that is the bedrock of moral action? So as to sidestep this difficulty in his portrayals of romantic love, Dickens often depicts a brotherly or fatherly attitude that is instant-aneously and conveniently transformed in due course into a marital relation: Walter and Florence Dombey in *Dombey and Son*, David and Agnes in *David Copperfield*, Arthur Clennam and little Dorrit in *Litte Dorrit*, Jarndyce and Esther in *Bleak House*, are all cases in point, where affection, first licensed by its familial form, is so absolved of any moral taint.

In the case of Bounderby, already morally bankrupt, no such difficulty arises. His relationship to Louisa is in fact a crude parody of the type of benevolent care that Dickens insists upon in his romantic portrayals. His desire, to be married to a beautiful young girl some decades his junior, with whom he has no intellectual or personal compatibility, shows a coarse sensuality – the sensuality to which Louisa reacts so strongly in the extract I cited – very much of a piece with the fundamental selfishness of his character.

The sex in *Hard Times* is concentrated in and around the figure of Louisa. Louisa is sexy, the object of desire both to Bounderby and Harthouse (and thus the means by which Dickens illustrates their commonality). From early on, her brother Tom is aware of her sexual allure:

Father has brought old Bounderby home, and I want you to come into the drawing-room. Because if you come, there's a good chance of old Bounderby's asking me to dinner; and if you don't, there's none.
(I, ix)

Later, he blames his turning to crime on his sister's withholding of her sexual favours: "Leaving old Bounderby to himself, and packing my best friend Mr Harthouse off" (III, vii). Louisa's sexuality is the means by which Dickens exposes what he takes to be the full implication of the materialism to which the Gradgrindian philosophy stands committed. The denial of spiritual nourishment leads to the ascendancy of the physical; at the most basic level, to the pursuit, without check or control, of merely bodily pleasure. This is the kind of vicious sensuality that Dickens ascribes to James Harthouse – "The man who, by being utterly sensual and careless," as he sums it up in his working plans, "comes to very much the same thing in the end as the Gradgrind school."

Harthouse's seduction of Louisa is motivated solely by selfish desire, whose object is made the more attractive by its being difficult to attain. The sensual gratification that he seeks, without regard to its consequences for his victim, falls in naturally with the pursuit of material gain advocated by the Gradgrindian scheme. Materialist thinking, at least as Dickens perceives it, contains no principles that might check men from acting on their desires, or that might safeguard the women whom they target.

The cost of sex – of unlicensed male desire – is a woman's reputation, her place in society, and, in this sense, her life. The fallen woman, as Dickens presents her, is on the road to prostitution. Simply by entertaining Harthouse's advances, Louisa, though remaining chaste, is removed to a kind of limbo; neither maiden, spouse, nor widow, she is consigned to that border-land in which awareness and desire remain untranslated into action. In *Hard Times*, the adulterous sexual act – meditated, but never finally achieved – remains at the conjunction, which only just fails to happen, of the moral vacuum created by Louisa's Utilitarian education and the materialism of her careless seducer.

Is Louisa in love with James Harthouse?

Louisa herself anticipates and answers this question, telling her father, with quiet desperation: "But if you ask me whether I have loved him, or do love him, I tell you plainly, father, that it may be so. I don't know" (II, xii).

James Harthouse is the object towards which Louisa's yearning for love – her desire for what, till then, she has neither experienced nor elicited – is perversely turned, an object that she knows to be unworthy, but to which she is still drawn, because it is all that is available. The awareness both of his unworthiness and, notwithstanding this, her attraction towards him, is captured in the tableau presented to Mrs Sparsit, the tableau of Louisa's utter immobility as she yields to Harthouse's embrace: "it was remarkable that she sat as still as ever the amiable woman in ambuscade had seen her sit, at any period in her life. Her hands rested in one another, like the hands of a statue." This, for all Louisa's stillness, is a seduction scene. In the next sentence, "Mrs Sparsit saw with delight that his arm embraced her" (II, xi).

Harthouse is the means by which the emotions so long stifled in Louisa are brought to the point of implosion and, inevitably, self-destruction. As the narrator comments in the aftermath of the crisis:

All closely imprisoned forces rend and destroy. The air that would be healthful to the earth, the water that would enrich it, the heat that would ripen it, tear it when caged up. So in her bosom even now; the strongest qualities she possessed, [had] long turned upon themselves. (III, i)

The sense of an impending catastrophe is present from Dickens's first introduction of his heroine to the reader, her downfall portended from the outset in the recurrent indications of an unnatural and unhealthy restraint:

There was an air of jaded sullenness... particularly in the girl: yet, struggling through the dissatisfaction of her face, there was a light with nothing to rest upon, a fire with nothing to burn, a starved imagination keeping life in itself somehow, which brightened its expression. Not with the brightness natural to cheerful youth, but with uncertain, eager, doubtful flashes, which had something painful in them... (I, iii)

As Louisa grows older, this starved imagination, this suppressed spiritual energy, already described here as a potentially dangerous "fire", is identified with her femininity, or, synonymously, the longing for love and domestic fulfilment, a longing that emerges, for instance, in her questions to Sissy about the relationship between Sissy's parents.

> *Louisa asked these questions with a strong, wild, wandering interest peculiar to her; an interest gone astray like a banished creature, and hiding in solitary places. (I, ix)*

The metaphor, with its implications of lawlessness and secrecy, again foreshadows later developments. The femininity that should have been domesticated into a loving marriage and, eventually, motherhood, is, by its repression, turned into something altogether more deviant and less manageable.

Louisa herself draws the parallel between her own personality and the smoking chimneys of Coketown: "There seems to be nothing there but languid and monotonous smoke. Yet when the night comes, Fire bursts out, Father!" (I, xv). Harthouse's arrival is the coming of Louisa's night, the condition under which the "Fire bursts out". Throughout, fire is Dickens's unsubtle metaphor for what is repressed in Louisa, her perpetual fire-gazing signifying her own awareness of the repression, of a feminine nature, that, untamed, becomes a dangerous combination of passion, resentment, and, finally, sexual excitement.

Harthouse is the catalyst for the explosion because his attitude and character are of a kind to which Louisa is especially drawn. In Louisa's attraction to Harthouse, Dickens underscores the point that the materialism entailed by a fact-based philosophy is finally equivalent to, or indistinguishable from, the materialism of a pure selfishness. The first produces, in Louisa, a spiritual emptiness and consequently a cold indifference to all but her brother; the second produces, in Harthouse, a chronic condition of ennui. Louisa recognises and responds to this affinity; to the counterpart, in Harthouse, to what she already sees in herself. As she describes it to her father, she found Harthouse

> *avowing the low estimate of everything, that I was half afraid to form in secret; conveying to me almost immediately, though I don't know how or by what degrees, that he understood me, and read my thoughts. I could not find that he was worse than I. There seemed to be a near affinity between us. (II, xii)*

This second conversation between Louisa and her father extends and completes that other, earlier exchange, in which she is brought to accept Bounderby's marriage proposal. At that time, her reiterated question – "What does it matter?" – presages her subsequent contemplation of

Jacqueline Tong as Louisa in the ITV serial (1977)

elopement and social disgrace. The attitude of perpetual weariness and indifference, the consequence of her Utilitarian upbringing and education, assumes in Harthouse the more dangerous, liberating, and alluring form of a release from moral and societal restraint. For Louisa, the transition from the first to the second is almost – almost, but not quite – inevitable.

Is cleverness unwomanly?

In his characterisation of Sissy Jupe, Dickens implies that her inability with figures and computation, and her difficulties with factual knowledge, are the necessary corollaries of her warmth and loving kindness, her ability to produce domestic comfort and harmony. Equally, Louisa's intellectual attainments are, it is suggested, at the expense of these other, more womanly attributes, with which Sissy is so amply endowed.

The contrast may be generalised more broadly. In Dickens's portrayal of women, the pursuit of learning and intellectual skill – academic, theoretical, mathematical – as an end in itself, or without reference to the domestic sphere, precludes the capacity for emotional nourishment and domestic order that belongs peculiarly to women. In this respect, Dickens endorses the model for women's learning that John Ruskin goes on to set out more formally in his now infamous lecture, "Of Queens' Gardens", published in *Sesame and Lilies* (1865):

> All such knowledge should be given her [the woman] as may enable her to understand, and even to aid, the work of men: and yet it should be given, not as knowledge, – not as if it were, or could be, for her an object to know; but only to feel, and to judge.

Louisa's education directly contradicts the Ruskinian model. Her acquisition of knowledge has been made an end in itself, without reference to the development of her womanly potential for feeling, or domestic harmony and order, or spiritual sustenance. By contrast, Florence Dombey in *Dombey and Son* is a paradigmatic instance of a young girl who gains knowledge of the kind and with the purpose later identified by Ruskin as "womanly", studying the books that are set for her brother, so that she might help him to learn:

> And high was her reward, when on Saturday evening, as little Paul was sitting down as usual to 'resume his studies,' she sat down by his side, and showed him all that was so rough, made smooth, and all that was so dark, made clear and plain, before him.

In *David Copperfield*, Agnes Wickfield, though she does not go to school, shows, similarly, an aptitude for book-learning, as David recognises: "when I brought down my books, [she] looked into them, and showed me what she knew of them (which was no slight matter, though she said it was)". But, here again, Agnes's intelligence is only an aspect of her genius for domesticity; she is first and foremost the "little housekeeper" – and on this ground, superior to Dora, who is hopeless at housekeeping. David outgrows Dora; in Agnes, he finds his ideal.

For Dickens, domesticity is the marker of an authentic and ideal femininity, with which intellect has little to do. In *Bleak House*, Esther Summerson, another exemplary house-keeper, wears her bunch of house-keys like a badge of identity, and repeatedly assures the reader that she is "not clever". In *Hard Times*, comparably, Sissy, whose talent for domestic order corresponds exactly to Esther's, is also emphatically "not clever"; so too Rachael, who, like Sissy, produces cleanliness, comfort, and order in the meanest of dwellings. Dickens's emphasis for women, like Ruskin's, is on emotional, rather than academic intelligence; intellectual ability and the acquisition of knowledge are important only insofar as they foster and nourish the first. The woman's object, as Ruskin puts it, is not to know, but to feel and judge, and Dickens's idealised heroines excel in this kind of feeling and judgement.

Thus Dickens plays down the importance of academic ability for women, but nonetheless celebrates in them intelligence of another order, the kind of intelligence which Sissy and Rachael possess so plentifully, and which is conspicuously absent, for instance, in Mrs Gradgrind. If Louisa's considerable intellect indicates a proportionate capacity – tragically undeveloped, as the novel depicts it – for emotional and moral strength, her mother, by contrast, is devoid of both. Mrs

Gradgrind is no more than a silly woman, whose weakness of mind makes her wholly inadequate as a wife and mother. Her barren and cheerless home represents not only a domestic fiasco but also, and synonymously, a moral failure, established immediately on her first appearance, in the terms in which she is described:

> *Mrs Gradgrind, weakly smiling, and giving no other sign of vitality, looked (as she always did) like an indifferently executed transparency of a small female figure, without enough light behind it. (I, iv)*

The indifference, the transparency, and the smallness are all damning. We might recall, by contrast, the introductory description of Sissy, irradiated by sunlight, or the later description of Rachael with Stephen: "the light of her face shone in upon the midnight of his mind" (I, xiii). The poorly-lit Mrs Gradgrind is in all respects their antithesis. Lacking womanly strength and efficacy, she is merely feebleness personified. Barely showing the signs of vitality in life, she gradually fades away into death.

Feminine power – or the strength that is the opposite of Mrs Gradgrind's feebleness – inheres in the feeling of which women are especially and naturally capable. To Dickens, as we have seen, feeling is fundamental to moral action.

Necessarily, then, women, as the repositories of feeling, are at the centre of his moral vision.

Although his fiction celebrates, and seeks to develop, men of feeling, it is women who are presented as instrumental in that development, and who guarantee the survival of feeling in a Utilitarian world. Hence the importance given in *Hard Times* to Sissy, whose perpetual mission is one of reparation and healing. Sissy transforms Gradgrind's cheerless household into a loving home, and she restores to Louisa her womanly identity, her natural capacity for warmth and emotion. As Gradgrind comes gradually to recognise, "some change may have been slowly working about me in this house... what the Head had left undone and could not do, the Heart may

ASTLEY'S CIRCUS

In 1768, Philip Astley (1742-1814), an ex-cavalryman, began to perform riding stunts for a paying public at his riding school on Westminster Bridge Road in Lambeth. In his trick riding, Astley rode in a circle rather than a straight line, an innovative new practice that was later to lead to the coinage of the term "circus" by a rival.

Soon Astley's establishment began to attract increasingly large audiences. Destroyed more than once by fire in the years that followed, it was built and rebuilt with growing opulence, becoming, in due course, "Astley's Royal Amphitheatre". It was Astley who established the 42-foot have been doing silently" (III, i). Sissy's moral stature and the full extent of her power are finally displayed in her confrontation and overpowering of Harthouse:

> *The child-like ingenuousness with which his visitor spoke, her modest fearlessness, her truthfulness which put all artifice aside, her entire forgetfulness of herself in her earnest quiet holding to the object with which she had come; all this, together with her reliance on his easily given promise – which in itself shamed him – presented something in which he was so inexperienced, and against which he knew any of his usual weapons would fall so powerless; that not a word could he rally to his relief. (III, ii)*

diameter size – the optimum required to generate the centrifugal force that a rider needed to balance on horseback – that has remained the standard for the circus ring ever since.

Initially, Astley's acts simply combined displays of equestrian skill with comedy routines, particularly spoofs of "bad" riding. Soon, however, pursuing the edge over his competitors, he began to incorporate other kinds of performances from London's streets and fairgrounds: jugglers, acrobats, clowns, strong men, and performing animals. Peter Cunningham's *Handbook of London Past and Present* (1850) also mentions "transparent fireworks, slack-rope vaulting, Egyptian pyramids, tricks on chairs, tumbling". Astley acquired an international reputation, and (according to the *Encyclopaedia Britannica*) went on to establish permanent purpose-built

(That Sissy's language to Harthouse "is the language of a Lord Chief Justice, not the dunce of an elementary school in the Potteries" is, as George Bernard Shaw points out, "only a surface failure".)

Quite apart from Dickens's impossibly idealised heroines, such as Rachael and Sissy, moreover, womanly feeling is also manifest in a whole host of ordinary, sometimes comical women who recur throughout his fiction. In *Hard Times*, they are such women as Mrs Pegler and the women of the circus, who, in taking leave of Sissy, "brought her bonnet to her, and smoothed her disordered hair, and put it on. Then they pressed about her and bent over her in very natural attitudes, kissing and embracing her... and were a tender-hearted,

circuses in cities across Europe."Sleary's Horse-Riding", then, reflects the equestrian origins of the circus.

Travelling circuses, also featuring equestrian acts, were numerous in the middle of the 19th century, but Paul Schlicke, in his extensive studies of Dickens and popular culture, argues that Dickens's "image of Sleary's circus is drawn more from his acquaintance with Astley's than with a travelling show". Sissy's father's routine, as "Mr. William Button, of Tooley Street, in 'the highly novel and laughable hippo-comedietta of The Tailor's Journey to Brentford'" (I, iii), reprises Philip Astley's best-known act, as "Billy Buttons", now recognised as the first circus clown, in a skit called "The Tailor of Brentford".

Later on in the book, Sleary predicts of his three-year-old

simple, foolish set of women altogether" (I, vi). The single detail of the bonnet and smoothed hair here emphasises the womanly talent for domesticity.

So thorough is Dickens's identification of feeling and femininity, indeed, that even Mrs Gradgrind, in her last extremity, reveals a long-suppressed womanly perception of a lack in her daughter's life, to which the dying woman remains tragically unable to put a name: "there is something – not an Ology at all – that your father has missed, or forgotten, Louisa... I want to write to him, to find out for God's sake, what it is" (II, ix). Louisa's temptation and near-fall is made deliberately to follow upon the death of her mother.

In his exaltation of feeling as the exemplary

grandson: "if you don't hear of that boy at Athley'th, you'll hear of him at Parith" (III, vii). Astley's – or the circus in general – was associated by Dickens with childhood delight and thus with innocent pleasure, as is made clear in the nostalgic portrayal, "Astley's", in his first-published book, *Sketches by Boz* (1836):

"there is no place which recalls so strongly our recollections of childhood as Astley's... For ourself, we know that when the hoop, composed of jets of gas, is let down, the curtain drawn up for the convenience of the half-price on their ejectment from the ring, the orange-peel cleared away, and the sawdust shaken, with mathematical precision, into a complete circle, we feel as much enlivened as the youngest child present." ∎

response, and domesticity as the exemplary quality of women, Dickens might certainly be said to corroborate the long-established patriarchal convention, dating from classical antiquity, of the "separate spheres" of the sexes – the convention, that is, which dictates that women are emotional beings, whose natural location is the domestic circle, where men are rational beings, who belong in the public arena. The unpalatable aspects, to a modern reader, of Dickens's gender stereotyping are not to be dismissed or explained away. But perhaps we might allow, nonetheless, that the misogyny associated with the "separate spheres" convention is hardly in evidence in his fiction, nor is the separation absolute. The womanly power that Sissy manifests can valuably be exercised, as her confrontation of Harthouse shows, well beyond the narrow sphere of the home. Sissy takes the place of – and compensates for – Louisa's inadequate male "protectors": her father, her husband, her brother. Later on, it is her intelligence and quick thinking that sends Tom to the circus, to avert his imprisonment and lasting disgrace.

More generally, indeed, the whole of *Hard Times* is precisely a critique of a certain kind of male rationality, presented here as inadequate, barren and ultimately destructive. In this context, if feeling is naturally gendered as female, Dickens's

advocacy of a morality of feeling might be said to be an argument for a more widespread feminising of society. So far as he argues, as he does throughout his fiction – although most explicitly in *Bleak House* – that the model of good house-keeping may and ought to be carried well beyond the home, into society and government, he may be said himself to destabilise – perhaps despite himself – the easy separation of the male and female spheres.

What's the point of the circus?

In much of Dickens's fiction, and most notably in *Bleak House*, domestic harmony, with an idealised heroine at its centre, is presented as the utopian alternative to the mayhem of a dysfunctional society. In *Hard Times*, this kind of domesticity, bringing about a sense of order in the face of the "muddle" of which Stephen Blackpool is so painfully aware, is briefly glimpsed in the transformation wrought by Sissy in Gradgrind's house, or by Rachael in Stephen's. More forcefully, however, and more radically, Dickens chooses to counter the cold rationalism of the Utilitarian world not by an alternative model of order, but by the disorderly, chaotic world of the circus. Already in his previous work – in the portrayal of the theatre troupe in *Nicholas Nickleby*, for instance, or the travelling waxworks show in *The Old Curiosity Shop* – Dickens had located in the sub-culture of popular entertainment the quality of loving kindness so conspicuously absent in mainstream society. Here, in *Hard Times*, that sub-culture, precisely because of its anarchic tendency, its resistance to systematisation, is celebrated as the antithetical pole of Utilitarian thought.

That the circus – devoted, as Dickens represents it, to pleasure, escapism, and the pursuit of 'Fancy' – is the antidote to inexorable 'Fact' – and, on this basis, the breeding-ground for the affections of the heart – is a point which hardly needs to be laboured. Nonetheless, and especially in the light of the widespread modern distaste for the use of animals in entertainment – in a 2012 article in The Guardian, the well-known Rastafarian poet, Benjamin Zephaniah, described it as "a modern-day slave trade" – a closer scrutiny is still necessary of the relationship between the circus, as Dickens represents it, and 'Fancy', his shorthand for the habits of thought antithetical to the Utilitarian view.

The idea that imagination is the origin of our capacity for sympathy is central to the 18th-century moral philosophy whose influence on Dickens I have already noted. Our imaginations take us out of ourselves into the situations and feelings of others, and, in so doing, in making us feel for others, become the primary instruments of moral action. This is the version of imagination developed in *Hard Times*. Purposely adopting its humbler synonym, "Fancy" – more euphonically polarised, too, from Utilitarian "Fact" – Dickens makes the circus a means for its large-scale cultivation. His radical innovation, in his depiction of the circus, is to take the cultivation of imagination – perceived, by his 18th-century predecessors as a process of gradual mental refinement, based on education and the appreciation of the fine arts – out of the realm of the elite, and make it more generally available across social strata.

The importance of the circus to Dickens is that it is a form of popular entertainment, and thus a broad means by which the ordinary individual's Fancy (or, to use another of his synonyms, 'wonder') can be nourished and stimulated. In his useful study of the subject, *Dickens and Popular Entertainment* (1985), Paul Schlicke notes the inextricable connection between Dickens's function as a successful popular entertainer – "the most widely popular English writer since Shakespeare" – and his celebration and defence of popular entertainment throughout his writing. In *Hard Times*, in particular, mass amusement – or, as Dickens perceived it, shared amusement –

presents the collective in its best, and indeed its only acceptable version: as a community. The circus, providing such amusement, is itself such a community – its members showing "an untiring readiness to help and pity one another" (I, vi) – and, by bringing people together in way that stimulates their Fancy, generates and enlarges that community. The more patent the disguises adopted by its performers – the "curls, wreaths, wings, white bismuth, and carmine" required to present Kidderminster as Cupid, for instance – the greater the testament to the good nature that is moved by it.

In taking as its purpose the bringing of pleasure to the mass of humanity, the circus becomes the preserve of common human decency. To emphasise the antithesis, Dickens divests the circus of anything that might be associated with the monotonous regularity of the Utilitarian view. Deliberately to polarise it from the schoolroom, then, with its "inclined plane of little vessels then and there arranged in order" (I, i), or from Mr Gradgrind's "lawn and garden and infant avenue, all ruled straight like a botanical account-book" (I, ii), the narrator insists that its members are "not very tidy in their private dresses" and "not at all orderly in their domestic arrangements" (I, vi).

Challenging the straight lines of the Utilitarian view, the physical appearances of the performers are invariably marked by a lack of proportion, or some other quality of the deviant and unregulated. Thus Mr Sleary, has "one fixed eye, and one loose eye, a voice (if it can be called so) like the efforts of a broken old pair of bellows, a flabby surface, and a muddled head which was never sober and never drunk". Mr E.W.B. Childers's "legs were very robust, but shorter than legs of good proportions should have been. His chest and back were as much too broad, as his legs were too short... he looked the most remarkable sort of Centaur, compounded of the stable and the play-house." Kidderminster, in turn, "a diminutive boy with an old face", confounds the orderly distinction of youth and age.

The association of absurdity with good nature, embodied elsewhere in some of Dickens's most memorable characters, here characterises a whole community. At the same time, the reader is exposed, too, to Sleary's propensity to drink, to the elaborate make-up required to disguise Kidderminster's age, to the bitter and sorrowful clown, Signor Jupe, Sissy's father. The dog "Merrylegs", in another characteristic instance of dissociative metonymy, is allied not with merriment, but with sadness and loss, shown beaten and bloody in the arms of the weeping clown, and towards the end, "in a very bad condition... lame, and pretty well blind" (III, viii).

Thus Dickens is at some pains to emphasise that the circus is no more than ordinary, and that the good nature of its members is the attribute of an ordinary humanity, far removed, in this respect, from the impossibly idealised goodness of Sissy or Rachael. Of the latter, it might well be said, as Fred Kaplan does, that they represent "his efforts to provide moral paradigms in his fiction to compensate for their absence in society". But in the circus, at least, Dickens finds the "the every-day virtues of any class of people in the world" (I, vi). And tellingly, the last word on Utilitarianism is spoken, not in the tone of resounding moral indignation, nor that of sentimental sweetness, but by the voice of the circus proprietor, slurred and thickened by his calling and by drink:

"It theemth to prethent two thingth to a perthon, don't it, Thquire?" said Mr Sleary, musing as he looked down into the depths of his brandy and water: "one, that there there ith a love in the world, not all Thelf-interetht after all, but thomething very different; t'other, that it hath a way of ith own of calculating or not calculating" (III, viii).

What can we learn from the novel today?

In the penultimate chapter of *Hard Times*, Bitzer delivers to his former teacher and mentor a succinct summary of the principles on which he has been educated:

> *"I am sure you know that the whole social system is a question of self-interest. What you must always appeal to, is a person's self-interest. It's your only hold. We are so constituted." (III, viii)*

This version of an extreme individualism, where each person is confined strictly by the parameters of personal interest and is incapable acting outside of it, is, as Dickens perceives it, at the centre of the social and economic systems that he targets throughout the novel. In opposition to it, he upholds another kind of individualism, where the locus of value is still retained in the individual, but that individual is differently conceived: not automatically propelled in the direction of self-interest, but capable of spontaneous feeling, naturally reaching beyond the self, to the other. Against the autonomous self, he sets the engaged self; against the collective, the community.

Compellingly, *Hard Times* shows us how this position – fundamentally, an ethical position – bears on the subject of representation, the subject, that is, of how we depict the world, or how we understand what "reality" might be. The principles of representation, both as Dickens describes them and as he deploys them in his own authorial strategies and techniques, are directly related to the ethical principles that he promotes. He identifies the devotion to the purely factual with the self-centred view posited by the Utilitarian and other materialistic systems of thought, arguing that its end result is not reality, but a distortion. By locating reality, instead, in shared experience, in the community of feeling that grounds the individual in his world, *Hard Times* displays its common basis with the realist fiction of the Victorian era. But at the same time, by its pronounced emphasis on feeling – in its avowal of, and determination to elicit the emotive, sentimental response – the text falls, contradictorily, into exaggeration and hyperbole, producing its own kind of distortion. The challenge for the reader is the negotiation of such contradictions.

In the course of such negotiation, the question that must arise for the reader of *Hard Times* is about the adequacy of Dickens's answers. To a large-scale problem of industrialisation – what Marx was to describe as the alienation of capital from labour – he offers a personal and local solution, and he offers the same solution, if one can call it that, to the related issue: the consequences of particular social, political, and educational principles for everyday human interaction and for human consciousness itself.

Marx and Engels, writing contemporaneously with Dickens, and passionately concerned, too, with the condition of the working classes, believed that the problem had to be, and could only be, countered by mass action. By contrast, Dickens's notion of an individual morality, grounded in each human being's capacity to feel, might well seem to raise more questions than it can possibly answer. As his contemporary, Richard Simpson, observed, the "disease of Coketown will hardly be stayed by an abstinence from facts and figures; nor a healthy reaction insured by a course of cheap divorce and the poetry of nature. In short, whenever Mr Dickens and his school assume the office of instructors, it is, as Stephen Blackpool says, 'aw a muddle! Fro' first to last, a muddle!'"

Simpson's dismissal cannot be easily gainsaid. And yet – in our own time, when the neat distinctions of left and right, and the sufficiency of any single system, are no longer altogether clear – there might remain something for us to consider in that troubled and tentative optimism that looks to a fugitive and unstable, but still persistent, human impulse as a touchstone for choice or action.

Hard Times and ethical criticism

Hard Times has been at the centre of the debate about "ethical criticism", whose leading proponent is the American philosopher and classical scholar, Martha C. Nussbaum. Nussbaum contends that literature can help foster the kind of sympathetic understanding necessary to enlarge the moral vision of the citizen and law-maker; the understanding, especially, of human beings in circumstances removed from our own. She posits a connection between the literary imagination and the responses of compassion and mercy, and emphasises the vital role played by the emotions in making good ethical judgements.

In Nussbaum's book, *Poetic Justice: The Literary Imagination and Public Life* (1995), she argues that literature conduces towards a "humanistic and multivalued conception of public rationality", that it offers, in other words, a more complex and rounded view of humanity, of human needs and desires, as the basis for the framing of public policy. On those grounds – the grounds that the insights granted by literary works can and should influence social policy – she commends particular, carefully chosen books for the imparting of what people 'need to learn as citizens'. Foremost among the three books she chooses is *Hard Times*, "which takes as its explicit theme the contribution of the novel to moral and political life, both representing and enacting the novel's triumph over other ways of imagining the world". *

Nussbaum's main opponent, Richard Posner, strenuously denies that literature has an ethical role. He proposes instead "the creed of aestheticism", arguing that "the moral content and consequences of a work of literature are irrelevant to its value as literature". Posner points out that many great works of the past are morally problematic in content, and, although he concedes that "literature is one path, though not the only path, to a better understanding of the needs, problems, and point of view of human types that we are unlikely to encounter at first hand", he denies that "a better understanding of people makes a person better or more just".

It might be said that Posner muddies the ground with the introduction of "aesthetics" into his argument. His fundamental objection is the ascription of a public function – the "inculcation of civic virtue" – to what he sees as something private: our choices of, and pleasure in, reading". To Posner, "*Hard Times* is a fine novel, because it is Dickens and has Mr. Bounderby; but regarded as a tract against economical thinking, it is shallow and easily refuted".

* *The other two novels chosen by Nussbaum are Richard Wright's Native Son (1940), and E.M. Forster's Maurice (written 1913-14; published 1971); the first for its portrayal of the experience of poor blacks in 1930s Chicago; the second, for its depiction of same-sex love in early twentieth-century England.*

The critics on Hard Times

"One excessively touching, heart-breaking passage, and the rest sullen socialism. The evils which he attacks, he caricatures grossly, and with little humour."
Thomas Babington Macauley (1854)

"We have seldom seen a more lamentable *non sequitur* than *Hard Times*. In short, the conclusion of the story is this: shut out all *Arabian Nights*, all imagination, fancy, poetry, from your schoolroom – rear your boy on the dry pabulum of facts and sciences, and your boy will rob the bank and become a dissipated little provincial scoundrel, as mean as he is guilty; whereas you have only to... have him trained among the delightful idealities of the circus to make everything that is kind-hearted, noble, and unselfish of this very boy."
Margaret Oliphant (1855)

"Dickens is always generous, he is generally kind-hearted, he is often sentimental, he is sometimes intolerably maudlin; but you never know when you will not come upon one of the convictions of Dickens; and when you do come upon it you do know it. It is as hard and as high as any precipice or peak of the mountains. The highest and hardest of these peaks is *Hard Times*."
G.K. Chesterton (1911)

"This is Karl Marx, Carlyle, Ruskin, Morris, Carpenter, rising up against civilization itself as against a disease, and declaring that it is not our disorder but our order that is horrible; that it is not our criminals but our magnates that are robbing and murdering us... the increase in strength and intensity is enormous: the power that indicts a nation so terribly is much more impressive than that which ridicules individuals."
George Bernard Shaw (1913)

"The story *Hard Times* has no other interest in the history of letters than that of its failure. At the time, even enthusiastic lovers of Dickens found it hard to read. At present they do not even try to read it. A large part of the book is mere trash; hardly a chapter of it is worth reading today".
Stephen Leacock (1934)

"I would suggest that the start of any critical wisdom about *Hard Times* is to dismiss every Marxist or other moral interpretation of the book. Yes, Dickens's heart was accurate, even if his notion of Benthamite social philosophy was not, and a great novelist's overt defense of imagination cannot fail to move us."
Harold Bloom (1987)

A SHORT CHRONOLOGY

1812 February 7 **Charles Dickens born at Southsea, near Portsmouth, second child and eldest son of John Dickens, an £80-a-year clerk in the Navy Pay office, and his wife Elizabeth. He was one of eight children, only five of whom survived.**

1815 Napoleon defeated at Waterloo.

1823 John Dickens, after being posted to London, is imprisoned for debt. Charles is sent to work in a boot-blacking factory off the Strand in London.

1827 Starts work as a solicitor's clerk in Gray's Inn, at a pound a week, but quickly begins to contribute to newspapers.

1836 First book of stories, *Sketches by Boz*, vivid snapshots of London, published to great acclaim. Marries Catherine Hogarth, daughter of a music critic.

1837 *The Pickwick Papers*, his first major success.

1838 *Oliver Twist.*

1850 Starts *Household Words.*

1853 October Twenty thousand cotton mill workers in Preston go on strike, demanding the restoration of wage cuts imposed by the owners in the wake of the trades depressions of the "hungry forties".

1854 January Dickens visits Preston and writes up his observations in an article in Household Words. In May the strike finally ends when the strikers give in, abandoning their demands.

1854 April to August *Hard Times* serialised in Household Words prior to publication.

1854 Dickens begins serialising Elizabeth Gaskell's novel about mill owners and workers in the north of England, *North and South*.

1858 Separates from his wife and the mother of his ten children after meeting the young actress Ellen Ternan, with whom he has fallen in love. Begins gruelling national tour, doing public readings of his work.

1859 Launches *All the Year Round* as a successor to *Household Words*.

1861 *Great Expectations*.

1867-8 Exhausting tour of America which nets him £19,000. By now he is afflicted with gout and his health is beginning to fade.

1870 June 9 Dies, while writing *The Mystery of Edwin Drood*. Buried in 'Poets' Corner', Westminster Abbey. He left £93,000 in his will.

BIBLIOGRAPHY

Brooks, Peter, "Dickens and Nonrepresentation" in *Realist Vision* (New Haven and London: Yale University Press, 2005).

Chesterton, G.K., "Introduction to Hard Times" (1908), rpt. in *Appreciations and Criticisms of the Works of Charles Dickens* (London: J.M. Dent, 1911), 169-77.

Collins, Philip (ed.), "Hard Times" in *Charles Dickens: The Critical Heritage* (1971; rpt. London: Routledge, 2009), 300-55.

Davis, Philip, *The Victorians: The Oxford English Literary History,* Vol 8. 1830-1880 (Oxford: Oxford University Press, 2002).

Dickens, Charles, 'On Strike' (Household Words, VIII, 11 Feb 1854, 553-9) rpt in *Selected Journalism* 1850-1870, ed. David Pascoe (London: Penguin, 1997), 452-66.

Glavin, John, "Dickens and Theatre" in *The Cambridge Companion to Charles Dickens*, ed. John O. Jordan (Cambridge: Cambridge University Press, 2001), 189-203.

Leavis, F.R. "Hard Times: An Analytic Note" in *The Great Tradition* (London: Chatto and Windus), 1948, 227-48; rpt. in *Hard Times*, ed. George Ford and Sylvère Monod (New York: W. W. Norton, 1966), 339-59.

Kaplan, Fred, *Sacred Tears: Sentimentality in Victorian Literature* (Princeton, NJ: Princeton University Press, 1987).

Levine, George, *The Realistic Imagination: English Fiction from Frankenstein to Lady Chatterly* (Chicago: Chicago University Press, 1981).

Miller., J. Hillis, "The Fiction of Realism: Sketches by Boz, Oliver Twist and Cruikshank's Illustrations" (1971), rpt in *Victorian Subjects* (New York and London: Harvester Wheatsheaf, 1990), 119-77.

Murdoch, Iris, *The Sovereignty of Good* (London: Routledge & Kegan Paul, 1970).

Nussbaum, Martha C., *Poetic Justice: The Literary Imagination and Public Life* (Boston: Beacon Press, 1995).

Posner, Richard A., Against Ethical Criticism: Philosophy and Literature 21.1 (April 1997), 1-27.

Schlicke, Paul, "Introduction: Dickens and the Changing Patterns of Popular Entertainment" and "Hard Times: The Necessity of Popular Entertainment" in *Dickens and Popular Entertainment* (London: Allen & Unwin, 1985), 1-13; 137-89.

The Oxford Companion to Charles Dickens (1999; reissued Oxford: Oxford University Press, 2011).

Shaw, George Bernard, "Introduction to Hard Times" (1913), rpt in *Shaw on Dickens*, ed. D.H. Laurence and M. Quinn (New York: Ungar, 1985), 27-35.

Solomon, Robert, *In Defense of Sentimentality* (Oxford: Oxford University Press, 2004).

Williams, Raymond, "The Industrial Novels: Hard Times" in *Culture and Society* 1780-1950 (1958), rpt. with a new introduction by the author (New York: Columbia University Press, 1983), 92-7.

INDEX

First published in 2015 by
Connell Guides
Artist House
35 Little Russell Street
London WC1A 2HH

10 9 8 7 6 5 4 3 2 1

Picture credits:
p.17 © General Images/UIG/REX
p. 31 © Philip Mould Ltd, London/Bridgeman Images
p.51 © ITV/REX
p.55 © ITV/REX
p.79 © ITV/REX
p. 89 © Private Collection/Bridgeman Images

A CIP catalogue record for this book is available from the British Library.
ISBN 978-1-907776-28-1

Design © Nathan Burton
Assistant Editors:
Katie Sanderson, Paul Woodward and Holly Bruce
Printed and bound in Malaysia

www.connellguides.com